Mutton Fish

Also from Aboriginal Studies Press

Bittangabee Tribe: An Aboriginal Story from Coastal New South Wales
Beryl Cruse, Rebecca Kirby, Liddy Stewart and Steven Thomas

Mutton Fish

The surviving culture of Aboriginal people and
abalone on the south coast of New South Wales

Beryl Cruse, Liddy Stewart and Sue Norman

Aboriginal
Studies
Press

First published in 2005 by Aboriginal Studies Press for the Australian Institute of Aboriginal and Torres Strait Islander Studies, GPO Box 553, Canberra, ACT 2601

The views expressed in this publication are those of the authors and not necessarily those of the Australian Institute of Aboriginal and Torres Strait Islander Studies.

© Beryl Cruse, Liddy Stewart and Sue Norman 2005

Apart from any fair dealing for the purpose of private study, research and criticism or review, as permitted under the *Copyright Act 1968*, no part of this publication may be produced by any process whatsoever without the written permission of the publisher.

National Library of Australia Cataloguing-In-Publication data:

Cruse, Beryl.

Mutton fish: the surviving culture of Aboriginal people and abalone on the south coast of New South Wales.

ISBN 0 85575 482 6.

1. Abalones — New South Wales — South Coast Region. 2. Aboriginal Australians — New South Wales — South Coast Region — History. 3. Aboriginal Australians — Food — New South Wales — South Coast Region. I. Stewart, Liddy. II. Norman, Sue. III. Title.

639.4832099447

Produced by Aboriginal Studies Press
Design and typesetting: Rachel Ippoliti, Aboriginal Studies Press
Map designed by Brenda Thornley
Printed in Australia by National Capital Printing

This project has been assisted by the Australian Government through the Australia Council, its arts funding and advisory body.

Front cover: (top) View of fish trap area at Mystery Bay, Narooma Region. (David Jefferies, *After 200 Years* project, 1989, AIATSIS Collection); (bottom) Shane Carriage with Keith Nye in background, cleaning mutton fish at Bateman's Bay, 1989. (David Jefferies, *After 200 Years* project, 1989, AIATSIS Collection).

To our children and grandchildren
and all future generations. This history is your story too.

Sue Norman, Liddy Stewart and Beryl Cruse
Eden, 2004

mutton fish / *noun*→abalone: a marine molluscus from the genus *Haliotis*. The meat is good tucker.

Contents

Preface	viii
Acknowledgements	x
Introduction	xi
Map	xiii
WALKUN	
A Day on the Beach	3
What the Middens Tell Us	7
MUTTON FISH	
Early Contact	15
Land	21
Livelihood	27
Life on the Beaches	33
ABALONE	
Put in for a Licence	57
Bag Limits	75
Court Cases	83
The Future	90
Glossary	105
References	107
Notes	108
Index	113

Preface

The impetus for this book began in 1993 when Beryl Cruse conducted an interview with her husband Ossie as part of her assessment for Aboriginal History as part of the Certificate of General Education (Year 10 equivalent) at Eden TAFE Annexe. In his interview Ossie told about gathering muttonfish from traditional times through to the present day. Ossie's story seemed so rich with meaning and possibilities for understanding, well beyond the usual histories of the local area that we (Beryl, fellow student Liddy Stewart and I) decided to undertake further research and to collect more oral histories.

Beryl's ambition was to record the history of those living on and from the south coast NSW beaches for her grandchildren and great-grandchildren. She could see that changes in access to beach camping and the limits to the coast's resources have restricted the younger generation's opportunities to experience the old beach culture.

For our research we searched through historical accounts of life on the south coast, reviewed archaeological surveys of middens and talked to many people who had memories of the south coast's beach culture. We were given a research grant from the Australian Institute of Aboriginal and Torres Strait Islander Studies and we are very thankful for that support. It enabled us to travel to other parts of the coast to speak to people there and to visit libraries in larger cities. It also gave us the encouragement to continue with the work through times of ill health and hardship.

Our first step was to look up the subject in various library catalogues. Immediately we saw the job was going to be harder than we'd thought.

There was almost nothing under the headings abalone or muttonfish or Haliotis. When we read the journals, papers and reports from ethno-historical and archaeological surveys of the area we found mutton fish mentioned merely as an aside: a '. . . moderate but uniform presence' in midden excavations and the occasional sighting of an '. . . ear shell beside a morass'.

How did this equate with the many oral accounts of the importance of mutton fish as a much desired, nutritious and plentiful food resource? It was, we decided, a matter of focus. Most writing on Aboriginal people is from a white perspective, a white focus. Non-Aboriginal eyes skim across the surface, missing clues and signs crucial for survival and meaning. As Albert Anunga says to Max Jones in Jones's book *Tracks* when asked if he could learn to read tracks the way that Albert did: 'We leave home just the way we are, no food, no guns, no tents. You learn very quick when you get thirsty and have no water and catch or find food.'[1] In other words give up your white cargo-cult support and step off into the real country.

Under the water mutton fish take on the colours, patterns and textures of the surrounding rocks and blend into the background. Seeing mutton fish is like trying to see the image behind the pattern in the 3-D magic-eye pictures. When you learn how to change focus, the image takes form, becomes solid and rises up toward you.

The story of the surviving cultures of Aboriginal people of the south coast of NSW is similar. It is there: solid, real and complex, but hidden from eyes that choose only to focus on the surface. We invite you to shift your focus to see and understand this story.

Sue Norman, 2004

Acknowledgements

The authors would like to thank the many people who helped us in gathering the information for the writing and production of *Mutton Fish*: Ernie, Beryl and Alan Brierly; Joe and Laurel Carriage; Andrew Chalk; Newton Carriage; Paul Hudson; Sarah Colley; Carol Cruse; BJ Cruse; Ossie Cruse; David Squires; Jean Squires; Ronald Nye; Ron and Vivienne Mason; Leo Ritchie; Tina Mongta; Darren Mongta; Doris Stewart; Ossie Stewart; Daneika Stewart; Stanley Nean and the Eden Office of NSW Fisheries.

We would also like to thank the Australian Institute for Aboriginal and Torres Strait Islander Studies for the research grant to help fund our work; Illawarra Institute of TAFE for study time and the Aboriginal Studies Press for taking on the manuscript for publication.

Illustrations

p. viii photograph by Ruth Maddison; **pp. 5, 11** drawings by Steven Thomas; **p. 16** Louis Auguste de Sainson, lithograph, 1833, National Library of Australia, nla.pic-an8148372; **p. 18** Oswald Brierly Journal p. 16, 1842, (ML-A535) State Library of New South Wales; **pp. 19, 32, 35, 37, 43, 44, 46, 60, 78, 92** photographs courtesy Sue Norman; **pp. 22, 26, 76** photographs by Ricky Maynard, *After 200 Years*, AIATSIS Collection; **p. 28** AIATSIS Collection; **p. 29** Old School Museum, Merimbula; **p. 31** courtesy Mitchell Library; **p. 51** photograph courtesy Esmay Cruse; **pp. 63, 69, 79** photographs courtesy Carol Cruse; **p. 89** *Sydney Morning Herald*, April 17-18, 2004; **p. 98** photograph courtesy Ty Cruse; **p. 103** photograph courtesy Shirley Thomas; **p. 104** photograph courtesy Lorraine Cunning.

Introduction

Mutton Fish is a story of the Aboriginal people of the south coast of New South Wales as told through the metaphor of *Haliotis*, or mutton fish. Easy to find and harvest, extremely rich in energy and accessible for as long as the beaches are freely open to all, this had always been a subsistence food. The Aboriginal people of south coast NSW have a long and complex relationship with the coastal environment that has nurtured them for many thousands of years. We hope to tell the story of this relationship and what has happened to the south coast people as their access to the coastal resources has been progressively restricted by European competition.

Haliotis is a type of mollusc or sea snail. There are seventy-five species known in the world and seven of these are found in southern Australian waters. In *Mutton Fish* the focus is on the *Haliotis ruber* or blacklip species found off NSW, around Tasmania and Victoria and across to South Australia. *Haliotis* are long-lived and prolific animals that feed exclusively on the algae and seagrass found on rocky reefs in waters up to twenty-five metres deep. They are mostly sedentary, developing a camouflaged colouring to suit their local environment, usually moving about and feeding at night to avoid predation by fish, manta rays and humans.

Haliotis has been known by many common names over time on the far south coast of New South Wales. The Nullica people of Twofold Bay called it *Walkun*, as recorded in the journal of George Augustus Robinson when he visited the area in 1844. The European explorers and settlers used the names *ear shell* and *mutton fish*.

Ear shell because its shape suggests an ear and *mutton fish* because the rich fatty meat smells and tastes similar to mutton. Some have suggested that *mutton fish* was originally coined by Kooris because *Haliotis* tastes similar to mutton flaps, a cheap cut of meat provided to Aboriginal people living on missions or working on farm properties. This name is still used by Kooris today. The Spanish American name *abalone* became widely used during the 1960s as the commercial exploitation and marketing of *Haliotis* intensified.

In this book we use the different names of *Haliotis* appropriate to the period in history being discussed. The first section, *Walkun*, looks at the pre-contact story of the Aboriginal use of shellfish resources. The section titled *Mutton fish* covers the period from contact to the 1960s. Finally, the section titled *Abalone* explores the changes since the 1960s as the mollusc came under intense demand. Licences and restrictions were imposed as the resource became scarce. Today live abalone is flown direct to Japan where it is sliced thinly while still alive and sold at astronomical prices.

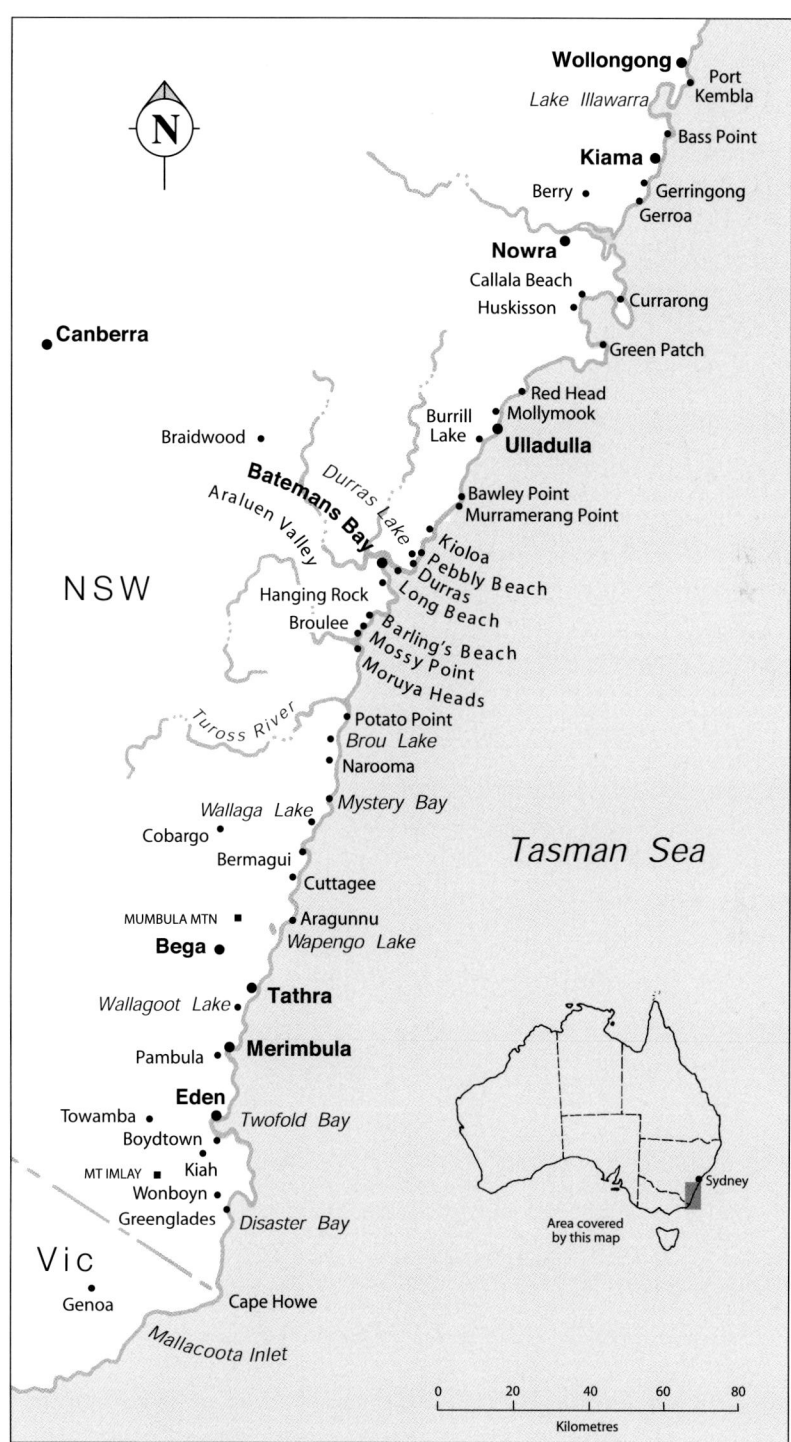

The south-eastern coastline of Australia

Walkun

A Day on the Beach

In the early morning light the first bright red streaks of sunlight rose above the sea mist created by strong seas churning and rolling, thrashing the shore. The light revealed one of the many beaches along the far south of the eastern NSW shores.

White cliffs cascaded into the high rising seas and waves broke against the numerous rocks nestled at their edge. This caused the heavy sea mist to rise to the tops of the cliffs. From there they crept steadily through the large trees and dense forest.

Along the wide beach the heavy waves crashed onto the sandy shore bringing with them huge pieces of seaweed, torn from the depths of the sea, to lie in great heaps on the shore. Seagulls screamed and cried out as they flew over the pieces of dead fish, crabs and sea urchins swirling in the water as it rolled onto the shore. The cold southerly wind blew the dry sand so that it rose like sprays of water along the beach that seemed to go on forever.

High above the mist a great sea eagle glided through the air searching for his first meal of the day. He rose high to the top of the cliffs, his loud screeching call mingling with the sound of the wind. From high above he could see the beach, where the sea rolled into the lake surrounded by thick forest, swamps and white sands. Further back the river curved into the forest and beyond to the mountains. The eagle's wings flapped and then stopped; the bird floated in the air in the strong winds. The cold winter was almost over but the harsh southerly winds still blew as if they would never end.

Just behind from the beach the morning light revealed the first stirrings as the men left the camp to hunt. They were going to the rich grassy flats up river to find the big mob of kangaroos and they had a long day's travel ahead. The women and children left the camp soon after. They headed for the beach carrying their babies and net bags, coolaman and digging sticks. The sticks, which had many uses, were made from strong wood hardened in the fire.

The children went with the women and were taught early in life how to hunt and collect food, catching small animals, lizards and birds, and having lots of fun doing it. They hunted as they walked along. As they reached the beach the women fished in the high tide. Their lines were made from plant fibre. To produce good strong string the fibre had to be freed from the plant tissue by being heated, soaked and beaten or sometimes chewed. The two-ply string was made by rolling the fibre along the thigh. Fish hooks were made from shell including walkun shell.

As they reached the rocks some of the women found the spots where they wanted to fish while others started to search for other foods around the rocks, collecting shellfish like mussels and pippies, found in the sand at the edge of the water. They searched by twisting their feet in the wet sand. The pippies rose to the top of the sand and were big and plentiful.

Crabs were collected by the children with lots of squealing and laughter going on. The fishing women were doing well, catching gropers, parrot fish and leather jackets and a good assortment of rock fish. They were good at fishing and happy with their catch. As they'd done well with the fishing they decided to have a feed. They gathered wood and made a fire near the rocks. As the flames died down they put their fish on the coals as well as the assortment of other seafood, crabs and small octopus that the children had caught. They all sat around, had a feast and then settled down while some dozed in the warm sun. When the children went for a swim and the babies slept the women talked and laughed, happy and content in this beautiful place.

The time moved on and the sea settled As the tide went out the women started to move. They had to keep gathering food for the evening meal, while the men would soon be back at the camp with what they'd caught during the day. Collecting their digging sticks, the women went to look for walkun, a favourite food that could only be gathered at low tide. Walkun are a big broad shellfish, a type of snail, which live in deep crevices and have to be prised off the rocks, which is what the women did with their digging sticks. At times they

Children gathering food from the shoreline

would feel for the walkun with their feet and then dive down and prise them off the rocks, but most times they were so plentiful they could just walk around at low tide and get large walkun. Even the children could get them this way. They only ever took what they needed to eat for the evening meal.

By early afternoon the women and children arrived back at the camp, having collected plenty of fish, shellfish, yams and vegetable food for the day. They gathered wood and rekindled the fires for cooking. Water was needed and it was collected in wooden containers that were taken to the spring and filled. Sometime later the men returned. On this day they had kangaroos and started to prepare them for cooking and sharing with the clan. Nobody went hungry in an Aboriginal camp; whatever was left over, the dingoes ate.

This time there was food for all, but at times the men would come back to camp empty-handed, for although there was plenty of game in the area it was sometimes difficult to catch. At these times members of the clan would live on what the women and children were able to gather. Fish, shellfish and vegetables are a much more reliable food source than the game and more often than not it would be the women who were the major providers.

Kangaroos were hunted in all areas, more often in the heat of the midday sun when they were drowsy and more easily caught. They were the largest animal hunted and were of great significance to the way of life of all traditional Aboriginal groups. They were a major source of meat, their bones were useful in making many implements and their skin was made into water carriers, rugs, cloaks, and babies were wrapped in or laid on the fur side of the skin. Strips of kangaroo fur were worn around the women's waist as a type of skirt or girdle.

As the food was being cooked the men went to their area, like a workshop, where they mended their hunting implements and equipment. For instance, replacing a barb on a spear. This was made then placed on the spear shaft, tied with kangaroo sinew and stuck with a gum made from the grass tree. Other things that needed to be fixed or made, like carving out a bowl for one of the women or preparing an animal hide were done at this time.

Soon the food was ready and everyone gathered around to eat and enjoy. There was much talking and laughter; these were happy times. Yarns were told about the day; funny yarns. Once the children were full they ran off to play . The boys often played games where they practised their throwing skills, or toy spears were thrown at rolling targets, like fur rolled up and tied into a ball. They imitated the men with their hunting skills. The girls played string games and with stick dolls rolled in fur and decorated. They spent a lot of time with the older women, learning how to make baskets and bags.

The children were loved and protected and were taught at an early age about their culture and life. The elders of the tribe were looked after as they were important people who made the final decisions as to what happened in the clan. The elders knew all the laws and customs and they were treated with great respect.

As the children ran and played the men and women gathered into a group and different people got up to talk. There were screams of laughter as the story was told with the storyteller doing all the actions; telling stories about what happened that day. It was a good day and everyone was contented and happy.

What the Middens Tell Us

It's difficult to estimate the exact period of time in which walkun has been gathered and eaten on the south coast. The coast itself has been subjected to rising sea levels that began about 20 thousand years ago, at the end of the last ice age, when the sea was 20 kilometres further to the east. The sea reached its present levels about seven thousand years ago.[1] As the sea rose it spread into the river valleys and formed the complex coastline; made up of the many bays, inlets and rocky outcrops we have today. The rising water also covered any archaeological evidence in the form of old shell heaps or middens that could have told us about the use of walkun by the coastal people before that time.

For people living on the south coast at this time the rising waters would have been a disaster. Many of their familiar landforms would have disappeared and it is believed that they moved inland to avoid the rising water levels. The south-east coast of Australia has a comparatively narrow continental shelf and has suffered less disruption than other areas, such as in the Bass and Torres Straits, where the low flat plains joining landmasses of Australia to New Guinea and Victoria to Tasmania were completely flooded. There, thousands of square kilometres of land rich in game and other foods was lost and the huge fresh water lakes were flooded by the sea.

On the south coast the newly formed coastline came to support a large population through the rich resources of the forests, lakes, rivers and the sea. The people used canoes made from sheets of bark folded at the ends and they fished with multi-pronged spears, nets and traps. It is was believed that they were the first in Australia to use a fish hook made from the edge of a shell, ground into a hook shape.

Women used these hooks and lines either from rocky ledges or from canoes in sheltered waters.[2]

Early archaeological sites on the south coast are rare. One at Burrill Lake dates back 20 thousand years and another at Bass Point dates back 17 thousand years before present (BP) at its base. Both these sites would have been too far from the sea then to contain any rocky-shore species of shellfish. Over time the Bass Point site changed from being a stone working area to a coastal midden and walkun shells are found there in layers dating back to more than 3000 years.[3] The largest concentration of shell middens in Australia is found on the south coast of NSW and these show that the people ate a wide range of shellfish, including increasing numbers of mussels and oysters. Walkun shells are found in small but constant quantities in middens located near the rocky shelves where they were easily caught. The oldest find dates back to about 3700 years.[4]

Walkun gives a high rate of meat to shell weight, so it is an efficient source of food. It is available in all seasons and has been dived for in most weather conditions because the complex shapes of the bays and inlets on the south coast provided shelter, whatever the wind direction. In extreme low tide walkun could easily be picked off the weed beds and from under rocks. This would have provided a reliable food source for children fossicking on the beach while the adults hunted or fished nearby.

Elsewhere in Australia walkun was gathered wherever it was found. In Tasmania, walkun and lobster were major components of the diet. Women dove for minutes at a time and gathered both, putting them into woven bags held around their necks. There are many historical descriptions of the women's skill, speed and endurance in gathering these important foods. This is in contrast to other parts of Australia where there is rarely any mention of walkun or ear shell, as it was known to early explorers. Perhaps the interest in walkun-gathering in Tasmania was partly inspired by people's awe of women doing this difficult work.[5]

Archaeological evidence in Tasmania shows a curious shift in the use of resources from the sea. Historical accounts point to the complete lack of scale-fish in the diet of the Tasmanians and the middens reflect this, with fish bones being found only in the deeper, older levels of the middens, persisting to about 4000 years ago. At the same time the amount of walkun shells and lobster claws showed a dramatic increase. It's as if there was a complementary shift away from fish towards walkun and lobster. There are many theories as to what happened. These include the following: a cultural impoverishment leading to people 'forgetting' the technology of fishing; a catastrophic poisoning creating a taboo on fish; an increase in diving skill leading to a preference for the richer food source; and a stabilisation of the coastal features creating a habitat suitable for the growth of these species.[6]

Some archaeologists have argued that the shift reflected a change in the food-gathering roles of the men and women, resulting in diving being a purely female activity.[7] Similar events have been described on the south coast of NSW where the development of fish-hook technology seems to have allowed women to become fishers where previously only men used the fish spear. Women who spent more time fishing had less time for gathering shellfish and there is evidence of certain species of shellfish become rare in the middens at this time. Divisions of labour between men and women are described throughout Aboriginal societies everywhere, but the role of children is also important. Women look after the young children while gathering food and the children learnt from them how to get basic foods to ensure their survival. This means that all adults and most children had the skills to gather these foods. On the south coast walkun was gathered as a survival food by all and it was probably dived for by the men.

Different species of walkun or *Haliotis* have been gathered and eaten around the world. The *paua* of New Zealand was also prized for its beautiful lustrous shell and is still worked by jewellers today. On the west coast of the USA, abalone was a source of food for the many tribes living there. The *Tlingit* Indians of Alaska traded, at great expense, for the iridescent blue-green Californian abalone, using it to make ceremonial earrings and nose rings and inlays for carvings.[8] The only mention we have found of the use of walkun for ornamentation was a description of an Aboriginal woman from the Esperance district who had fastened her kangaroo skin cloak with:

> . . . a bit of mutton fish shell: . . . This had been rudely ground and was about two and a half inches long and two inches wide of a slightly curved shape, showing the pearly inside.[9]

The traditional use of walkun has been carried on into modern times in the Aboriginal communities of the south coast. This is apparent in the methods of fishing, processing and the practice of sharing amongst the members of the group. Ossie Cruse describes what his elders taught him:

> In traditional times when Aboriginal people gathered food from the ocean, particularly mutton fish, it was a cultural thing that took place, many many years ago . . . But we know that handed down from our forefathers, particularly from my dad and my uncles, they taught me how to gather mutton fish along the east coast of New South Wales, particularly the south coast. The mutton fish were gathered for food and many times we gathered them to trade.
>
> Beyond the times that we started gathering mutton fish, in more modern times, we know that our people always used to take mutton fish as a delicacy from the ocean. And there was a special way of processing mutton fish, . . . it was there on the rocks that the meat of the shellfish was taken out of the shell. And the shells was always left on the shoreline, on the tidal line. The mutton fish was pounded on the rocks there, it was pounded to tenderise, and taken home and cooked in various ways. That was the traditional way of processing mutton fish, to take it immediately out of the shell when you got it out of the water. If you allowed the fish to die in the shell it would get a lot tougher . . .
>
> Now when we took mutton fish home we shared with others, that was a traditional thing, people always asked you to bring a feed of mutton fish home with you. So long before we did that, it was practised by our people. Even our tribal people used to bring mutton fish home to share with the camp, particularly our older people who couldn't get into the water, who couldn't dive. And always it was a tremendous delicacy amongst our communities.[10]

Archaeological sites can only show material evidence and so they can only partly illustrate Ossie's statement. Midden sites on the south coast contain small but constant numbers of walkun shells, meaning perhaps that some were taken back to camp to share with the old people staying there. Sarah Colley, from the Department of Prehistoric and Historical Archaeology at the University of Sydney,

Methods of preparing walkun

has excavated an Aboriginal shell midden at Disaster Bay on the far south coast that shows continuous occupation well into this period. Sarah made a latex peel of the side of the dig into the midden and this, along with some of the items found in the midden, is on display at the National Museum of Australia in Canberra. She explained that you can easily recognise abalone in a midden by its shiny inner surface and patterned outer surface.

> **Sarah**: Most of the work that's been done on shell middens in New South Wales in the last few years has been done for environmental impact assessment work and that limits the type of study that gets done and . . . it's been interesting for me doing this project on the south coast because the site there hasn't been under threat from a development and it's meant that I've been able to spend more time on it and have been able to document it more carefully.[11]
>
> [This site] I've been working on . . . an excavation of a site down at Disaster Bay Wonboyn Lake area . . . It's a shell midden in a rock shelter and it's quite deep. I've had it radiocarbon dated . . . and I think people were using it from about six hundred years ago up until possibly the middle of the nineteenth century. . . . This site's really interesting because it's got deposits, which span the period between the archaeological and historical periods. . . . It's got abalone shells in it . . . they're all the way through. So, if you needed to provide material evidence that people were continually taking abalone, that's a really interesting

site because it spans the historical period and then you could link it into the documentary and historical accounts.

Sue: What sort of other material was in that historical period?

Sarah: Well, there's very little material that is European in origin but . . . I have an idea about the dates. Near the top of the site . . . there are three pieces of bottle glass, which date from the nineteenth century and we know that because of the colour of the glass and I've shown it to colleagues of mine who are specialists in historical archaeology who have confirmed the date. They're only very small fragments but there's one piece of glass which is flaked on both sides and it's obviously been shaped into some sort of tool, it's not just a piece of glass that's fallen on the ground and got chipped . . . It's interesting first of all because that site is a long way from any European settlement . . . Now that raises another question, when would Europeans have come in the area and what impact might that have had on Aboriginal lifestyles and that's not something that archaeology alone can say very much about. And that's why the study's really interesting because it could link into the historical studies of what happened to people when Europeans first came here. Was that glass something which was traded in or did people carry it there, and when did people stop using the site in the traditional manner? You know, that's really interesting stuff and I think it's really exciting because this is a whole new area of archaeology . . .
I think a lot of archaeologists have traditionally been interested in just looking at what happened before the Europeans came.[12]

In the next chapter we examine the historical accounts to find out what they say about the shellfish economy of the far south coast after Aboriginal contact with the Europeans and others.

Mutton Fish

Early Contact

The earliest accounts of contact between Europeans and the Kooris of the far south coast happened by way of the sea. The main transport route from Sydney to Tasmania and the rest of the world passed south along the east coast and around into Bass Strait. The meeting of two oceans and weather systems led to frequent storms and survivors of wrecked ships or those seeking shelter were the first Europeans to visit the coastline.

The first recorded contact was written in a journal by the survivors of the *Sydney Cove*, a trading ship travelling from Bengal to Port Jackson, which was wrecked on an island in Bass Strait in 1796. A party of seventeen men left in a long boat for Port Jackson but were run aground, this time on the coast of East Gippsland, and so they set out to walk to Sydney. On this journey they experienced many privations but were often assisted by the Aboriginal people they met on the way. This usually took the form of meals of fish and shellfish, which appeared to make up the major part of the local diet.[1] The journal mentions mussels by name but at times the generic term 'shellfish' is used leading one to guess that the species in these cases was unknown to the writer.

There are very few references to mutton fish in the early journals, but the descriptions of the methods of gathering point to their presence in the diet. In Sydney officers from the First Fleet kept records of their encounters with the local people. John Hunter described seeing men diving for shellfish in the surf and Bradley wrote an account of seeing shellfish being prised off rocks by means of a shell mounted on the end of a spear thrower.[2] In December 1817 a visitor to the south coast, Phillip Parker King, described the use of mutton fish shells as drinking vessels in Snug Cove, Eden:[3]

> ...on the banks of the morass (water source) were many *Haliotis Giganta* shells used by the natives as drinking vessels. Near the morass in the evening 3 or 4 natives were seen but ran away.

It is interesting to note the different observations when comparing accounts from other nationalities who visited the south coast. In 1826 the French courvette, *Astrolabe*, called into Jervis Bay as part of their scientific expedition around Australia. Despite the fact that the English settlers had been engaged in a bloody conflict with the local people for thirty years the French encounter was peaceful and profitable. A lithograph showing sailors and tribesman sharing catch of fish, by Louis Auguste de Sainson, depicts the people as healthy and well fed, joyously dancing and grabbing at the fish. The ship's surgeon and naturalist, Joseph Paul Gaimard, collected a vocabulary of about 180 words of the Jervis Bay language in which eighteen different species of shellfish are named. In the list all are individually noted in French while, in the English translation, some, including the word for mutton fish, are referred to by the generic term 'shell'.[4]

Sailors from the *Astrolabe* sharing their catch.

By the 1800 sealers were operating in Bass Strait. They left gangs on the islands to hunt seals while they transported skins to Sydney. Some stopped in Twofold Bay and there are a number of historical reports of conflict with the local people defending their women from the notorious kidnappers who took Aboriginal women to the islands as work and sex slaves. By the time settlers came to the area venereal and other diseases were evident amongst the people.[5]

Traditionally, south coast people travelled between the coast and the mountains to participate in large gatherings which centred on seasonal resources. In summer, groups would gather from the coast, Monaro and the alpine regions to share the masses of fatty Bogong moths which slept in caves at high altitudes. While there, the tribes would hold ceremonies, arrange marriages and trade. In the winter, people returned to the coast and large groups would rush to where a whale had stranded to feast on the massive creature.

Toward the end of the 19th century, a Thoorga speaking man told RH Mathews of a whale hunt:

> When the natives observe a whale, *'murirra'*, near the coast, pursued by killers, *'mananna'*, one of the old men goes and lights fires at some little distance apart along the shore, to attract the attention of the killers. He then walks along from one fire to the next, pretending to lame and helpless, leaning upon a stick in each hand. This is supposed to excite the compassion of the killers and induce them to chase the whale toward that part of the shore in order to give the poor old man some food. He occasionally calls out in a loud voice, *ga-ai! ga-ai! Dundya waggarangga yerri-maran-hurdyen*, meaning *'Heigh-ho! Heigh-ho! That fish upon the shore throw ye to me!*
>
> If the whale becomes helpless from the attack of the killers and is washed up on the shore by the waves, some other men, who have been hidden behind the scrub or rocks, make their appearance and run down and attack the animal with their weapons. A messenger is also dispatched to all their friends and fellow-tribesmen in the neighbourhood, inviting them to come and participate in the feast. The natives cut through the blubber and eat the animal's flesh. After the intestines have been removed, any persons suffering from rheumatism or similar pains, go and sit within the whale's body and anoint themselves with the fat, believing that they get relief by doing so.[6]

Early settlement on the far south coast was based on the whaling and pastoral industries and Aboriginal people were employed in both these fields as geographic isolation limited the availability of white

Native, Twofold Bay
Oswald Brierly,
1842.

workers. The European shore-based whaling industry took advantage of the traditional migration to the coast over winter. During the whaling season more than one hundred Kooris would be camped around Twofold Bay and some later lived in four huts at the Kiah inlet. The seasonal work suited them as it mirrored the winter coastal camps. Some travelled back to their tribal land in Victoria, inland or north up the coast when the season finished. The special relationship with the orca or killer whale continued into the early twentieth century and was taken up by the Davidson family whaling at the Kiah inlet. The life and death of one killer whale, called Old Tom, lead to the development of a whaling museum in Eden, now a major tourist attraction in the town.

This history of Aboriginal people working alongside white men is slowly becoming appreciated as part of Eden's pioneer past, as more evidence is found in old newspaper stories up to the start of the twentieth century.

> The killers have returned. The 1909 season is just opening. Mr Alex Grieg discovered on Tuesday morning they had returned — with a baby. It is proposed this baby should be christened Alex Grieg in compliment to an old whaler who first saw it. Others suggest it should be called Beggaree, after a darkie whaler who died here some time ago. The 'black' whalers believe that when they die they will return as killers.[7]

Another historical hero of the Eden area was Benjamin Boyd who used Twofold Bay in the early 1840s as the port for his large grazing estate on the Monaro and into Victoria. He was a charming 'entrepreneur and opportunist'[8] whose settlement, called Boydtown, started to fail when the depression of 1843 led to the collapse of the beef market. At this stage Boyd disappeared on a Pacific island while looking for Island labourers to bring back to Boydtown.

Boyd set up a shore-based whaling station in Twofold Bay and employed artist Oswald Brierly as the manager. Oswald Brierly lived near current-day Edrom for six years and took a keen interest in the local Aboriginal people. He kept a journal of his experiences which included some wonderful sketches of those he got to know as friends. He was very impressed in the Koori's skill. In 1842 he observed:

> The natives make very good whalers and many of them are employed by Imlay who gives them slops — provisions in return for their services . . . Their sight is better and they see the fish sooner than the white men . . . All the Twofold blacks are good boatmen, handling the oar with great skill and dexterity. The gins pull remarkably well.[9]

Ernie Brierly and his son Alan, at Moruya, 1998.

Today's south coast Aboriginal families have direct links to those who worked in the early coastal industries. One such family, still active in commercial fishing on the far south coast, are the Brierlys. Their name comes from Oswald Brierly who adopted an Aboriginal boy. As the Brierly family story tells it:

Beryl Cruse: Your mother and father, the old couple, they were fishing too.

Ernie Brierly: Yeah, down at Eden they were whaling ever since the game started. Dad's father, he was a whaler down there and Dad, he was fishing ever since that. Then I come up with my boys here; we're all generations now . . . Dad used to be the lookout man — they reckon nothing could get past him, he was good.

Beryl Cruse: What was your father's name?

Ernie Brierly: Walter, Walter Brierly. His [father] was Walter Oswald . . . We got a Pommy name, Sir Oswald Brierly see, he adopted Dad's father. Down at Eden at the whaling station there. Dad was bred and born at the mouth of the Kiah River under one of those trees with the berries on them, a mulberry tree. That's where he used to play around the mulberry trees. Just have to look at the *Killers of Eden*[10] and you see his name in there.[11]

Land

Access to land and resources for south coast Kooris came under threat as the white settlement on the south coast expanded. Favoured sites on rich river flats and lakes were taken in the late 1820s by pastoralists. On the shoreline, the best camping grounds were those with access to fresh water, diverse littoral forests for food, medicines and other materials, extensive rocky shelves and gutters for plentiful shellfish, and good lookout points for fish spotting. Large ancient middens reveal the extended use of such sites. Increasingly into the 21st century these sites have come under pressure with the expansion of fishing and tourist towns and Kooris have had to struggle to retain their access to their land, resources and for the continuation of their culture.

One such example is Murramarang Point between Bateman's Bay and Ulladulla. It is a headland with large rock platforms providing habitat for many fish and shellfish. Across a narrow passage from the headland is Brush Island which is surrounded by similar rock platforms. Just to the north is a brackish water lagoon, home to many visiting swans and other birds. This would have been a very rich environment for Aboriginal people.

Murramarang Point is now reserved as an Aboriginal site and has extensive middens showing long term occupation, going back about 3500 years. Nearby Brush Island was a mutton bird rookery during the season between September and April. The bones of these birds were used to make points for fish spears. George Bass landed on Brush Island in March 1797 and commented on the place as being frequented by natives.[1] The sand on the headland served as a storage for fresh water, and in 2000, we saw it seeping through onto the rocks at the sea's edge.[2] This would have been, as the National Parks and Wildlife Service interpretation board says: 'a place of food'. The integrity of the site was destroyed when the cattle brought in by settlers at Murramarang Station damaged the vegetation cover, leading to the erosion of the headland. Ironically, the large middens exposed by this erosion has allowed the study and appreciation of Murramarang Point as a place of significance for the Aboriginal people of the south coast.

It was places such as these, highly valued by the local people, which were more likely to be strongly defended against the squatters and their cattle. Conflict between settlers and Aborigines was widespread throughout Australia and there are veiled references to troubles and dark deeds at this time of Australia's history. Kooris fought to defend their country and many were killed.

> We will never know exactly how many Aboriginal people lost their lives in violent conflict with those who invaded their lands. Many died from smallpox, influenza and venereal disease, many died on the fringes of the fledgling settler encampments after they were displaced from their homelands. But it also true that significant numbers died in sporadic warfare, on rare occasions in massacres and sometimes from poisoning. Eden–Monaro was not settled 'peacefully'. Like many other areas of Australia, violent conflict was part of the story of 'settlement'.[3]

Midden in sand blow-out at Murramarang Point.

Most of these events have remained hidden from history, but one in particular has been recorded in detail in official documents. This is the case of a massacre of at least four Aboriginal people, shot in cold blood at the 'place of food', Murramarang Point.

In 1832 a shooting party of convicts and freemen, led by the overseer, Joseph Berryman, shot and killed two men, a young pregnant woman and an older woman known as Mene Mene in retaliation for spearing three cows and a working bullock. A witness to part of the incident, Hugh Thompson, reported the events to the authorities in Wollongong; who arrested Berryman. Later, officially questioning Thompson's state of mind and evidence, they released him without trial.[4] This lack of action endorsed the prevailing attitude that the land was there for the benefit of white settlers and Aboriginal people must not stand in their way.

On the south coast, pressure for land and resources intensified when the free selection Acts of 1861 opened land to a large influx of white settlers. This coincided with the development of goldfields in Braidwood and the Araluen Valley and many other small goldfields along the coast and hinterland. Gold mining continued up to the turn of the century, encouraging and supplementing the incomes of settlers who struggled to establish themselves on the river flats and surrounding hills.

The prevailing model of smallholdings for yeomen farmers provided an official framework for land claims by the Aboriginal people who attempted to retain parts of their traditional lands.[5] Amongst the earliest claims on the south coast were some in the Bodalla region. In 1872, senior Aboriginal men, Richard Bollaway, Merriman and Yarroro, began making formal requests to the Lands Department to select land around the mouth of the Tuross River. As these areas were already within the coastal reserve they were allotted to the men as 'permissive occupancies'. Continued insistence for secure tenure resulted in the land being registered as Aboriginal Reserves in 1877.

In 1882 the first official Protector of Aborigines was appointed. His task was to travel throughout New South Wales and record Aboriginal needs and demands.[6] Throughout NSW the dominant plea from Aboriginal people was for secure land, and so a process of granting reserves was established. Kooris used the reserve lands to farm, build secure housing and as a base for fishing. Within ten years many of these reserves had been cancelled or revoked as white settlers petitioned the Aboriginal Protection Board to gain access to Aboriginal land. The land on the Tuross, small lots of about 40 acres, was later revoked in 1914 and 1922 with the last, claimed by Merriman, revoked as late as 1969.[7]

Another example is land on Blackfellow's Lagoon at Kalaru, between Tathra and Bega. This reserve was granted to George Cohen in 1883 by the newly established Aboriginal Protection Board and is recorded in the Register of Aboriginal Reserves held in the NSW State Archives.[8] The report in the register describes the land as 100 acres, thickly timbered, badly grassed, six acres cleared and two under cultivation. George Cohen and his family, totalling twenty-seven people, lived there in 'a hut and a few gunyahs'. A white man, William Lavington, leased about an acre of the land, paying Cohen £9 a year and employing him as a fisherman. This situation continued for a number of years but after Cohen's death a further report, dated August 1890, observed the fences in ruin after a bushfire, with the hut occasionally occupied by an Aboriginal man, Jack Hoskins, his wife and two children. By April 1893 the land grant was revoked.

The reserves ensured there was always a widespread presence of Kooris along the coast, scattered amongst the growing white settlements. Their presence is now recorded in Land Department's records, reserve registers and in names of features on the landscape. Obviously, Blackfellows Lagoon refers to the people who lived and worked there on Cohen's reserved land. Close by, at the mouth of the Bega River, Black Ada's Swamp is named for the Aboriginal woman who sold reed baskets to travellers crossing the river in the punt.[9]

Expanding townships like Moruya, Ulladulla and Tomakin engulfed many small reserves on the coast. These reserves were revoked over the years, forcing the Kooris out to more remote campsites or onto the managed missions at Wallaga Lake or Roseby Park, near Nowra. In Bateman's Bay, Kooris fought to retain their land within the town, near their work at the local sawmills; and for their children to attend the public school. Jane Duren wrote to King George V to request that her grandchildren could remain at the school and to 'Let them stay on the land that was granted to them.'[10] The protests were successful and the land in the town was secured. In 1927 the Board revoked the out-of-town site where they had hoped to move the people.

As the twentieth century proceeded, the options for south coast Kooris were limited to living on the managed missions or camping on beaches or on the riverbanks. Some unofficial reserves were retained as family camping and fishing grounds, dating back well before white settlement. Ossie Cruse remembers the campsites he lived and worked at on the south coast:

Ossie: I mentioned there used to be a cultural gathering, and because it was a cultural gathering there was special sites that our people used to go and camp. Those campsites was all the way through from Wollongong right through to the Victorian border. Many of those campsites were on the shoreline where there was fresh water. I can still remember those sites, where they used to gather mutton fish, where the favourite spots where. Some beginning were as up as far as Hill Sixty at Port Kembla and some of the favourite camps were at Gerroa, Gerringong and Boat Harbour, Werri Beach, Minnamurra and Bass Point and East Beach at Kiama.

Then coming down the coast some of the favourite spots used to be places like, Currarong and Callala, Lamb's Point, Green Patch, Caves Beach, Kioloa, Red Head, Mollymook at Ulladulla, Myora and Bawley Point, Pebbly Beach, Point Upright, Durras, the mouth of Durras Lake, Long Beach at Bateman's Bay, Hanging Rock at Bateman's Bay, Barling's Beach and coming south to Potato Point and all the way down south there were these camp sites. Like Mystery Bay and down at Cuttagee, Cowdroy's, just little bit north of Tathra. They were all traditional campsites that our people used for many hundreds of years. Beautiful sites and they were beautiful places to visit.[11]

Beryl: But the families, some families still make it to the places where they used to camp. Even now, our family go out from Nowra, Kinghorn…Our family from up round Wollongong go there and Deila and Nancy and them. They still all go to that one place at Christmas.

Liddy: And that was the tradition for year and years. It's funny how the traditional thing goes on and on and you don't realise that you're doing it.

View of fish trap area at Mystery Bay, Narooma Region.

Beryl: Yes, and even Stewarts they'll come down from Sydney and camp down at Brou Lake, out from Bodalla. And they've been doing it for years. Different areas on the coast they still make back to go there.

Ossie: But the thing that I was always concerned, and still concerned about is that, one by one you would see the camping places fenced off, and 'No Camping' signs put up. Araganu was a really beautiful spot and but for Buddy Campbell taking a stand and camping there, living there, and other campers like him. They would have closed that area off.

Beryl: Yes that's another place they make, different family groups go to different areas.

Ossie: There are very few areas left to camp. If you go there camping you're facing a fine. So you've got to be careful where you go and camp. So it's all a stress because the way they they're drawing up laws, they're not talking to Aboriginal people. Because we just go out to get our food as we've always got it . . . We were talking about it at our last Council [NSW State Land Council] meeting, even inland rivers fishing, hunting and gathering, even the goanna. They get fined for it. They've got to hide their bush tucker; they've got to hide before they get fined. So it's crazy, the stress they're putting on people.[12]

Livelihood

> See we never, apart from a short time at Wallaga, lived on a mission under control of the managers and that's why we just cruised around. All the work that we did was basically either harvesting natural resources or working with the land in some other way. Like bean picking, seafood gathering, mill work.
> (BJ Cruse)[1]

Living off the resources of the land and, particularly, the sea, remained the mainstay for south coast Kooris throughout the development of the white settlement. Pre-contact methods of fishing and gathering have been handed down for generations through stories and songs, ensuring a continuing connection with the environment. As well the development of industries and agriculture on the south coast has relied on Koori labour. In turn, the experiences of this work has been absorbed into the more traditional lifestyle of fishing, camping and following the seasons.

In pre-contact times all activities were associated with songs and some remnants of these were recorded by Janet Mathews in the 1960s. They are now stored in the sound archives at the Australian Institute of Aboriginal and Torres Strait Islander Studies (AIATSIS) in Canberra. Percy Davis grew up in the Tuross River area on land preserved by the senior men in the 1870s. He was in his eighties when Janet recorded him singing the song of the westerly wind. The song calls on *Gurrugumar*, the westerly wind, to blow and flatten the seas so the fish can be caught. At about the same time Janet recorded Jimmy Little senior singing a song about gathering oysters, taught to him by his mother from Wallaga Lake.[2] Fishing and shellfish gathering continued to be an important part of the south coast livelihood well into the twentieth century.

Other records of this time have been preserved in the drawings and paintings of Mickey from Ulladulla. He lived in one of the town reserves and made a living from a mixture of hunting-gathering and trading with the white community. Mickey sold brooms from his camp and his drawings and paintings were in wide demand. Mickey drew the fishing, hunting and camp life as well as corroborees and the native fauna and flora. He also drew the sawmills around Ulladulla and Bateman's Bay.[3]

As the timber industry developed Kooris were employed all along the coast in sawmills and as sleeper cutters. They either camped in the bush or lived in houses made and furnished with mill off-cuts. Some families became known as mill workers, in particular the Stewarts who lived on the town reserve in Bateman's Bay where the main industry was saw milling. The forest and mill work was close to the favourite campsites on the beach where fish and shellfish could be gathered.

Mickey of Ulladulla's drawing of the river, with boat, fish, kangaroos and sawmill, c.1880.

Interest in mutton fish grew with the arrival of large numbers of Chinese coming to Australia for the gold rush. They first landed at Twofold Bay in 1855 and walked to goldfields, thereby escaping the £10 head tax imposed to discourage Chinese miners from entering Victoria.[4] Mutton fish was considered a delicacy in China and the gold miners were quick to set up fishing and trading businesses to meet the growing demand. The Chinese and Aborigines shared the stigma of racial prejudice and there are many instances of inter-marriage and association between the two groups. In New South Wales, Chinese entrepreneurs set up fishing and fish drying operations in the 1860s just north of Sydney to supply the goldfields. Aboriginal people were employed to collect mutton fish for these traders.[5] At this time, Chinese entrepreneur Ah Chouney was reported to have owned up to twenty boats, employing mainly European crews. It is said that mutton fish were depleted from the Palm Beach area due to the number of boats and demand caused by the widespread use of the shell for shirt buttons.[6]

The Chinese who stayed on in southern Australia after the gold rushes lived by working as market gardeners and as herbalist doctors. Both occupations were in great demand in rural areas where medical help was very scarce and people who lived in towns relied on the Chinese gardeners for fresh vegetables. Some continued the mutton fish trading businesses set up in the days of the gold rush on the far south coast, which continued to be lucrative. Aboriginal people were able to use their traditional diving skills and their extended family labour in their beach camps to work with the Chinese, right along the south coast.

Doctor Ah Yeck pictured in Pambula at the turn of the last century.

Mutton Fish

Ben and Sarah Cruse and their son Ossie describe the process as they remembered from the past:

Ben: While I was at Mogo an old Chinaman [Ah Chin] came up to me looking for someone to drive his truck. And so he got me then to go to a market garden, the other side of Bateman's Bay, place called Kioloa where he had a market garden and he used to get abalone . . . We used to dive for abalone, me and this old Chinaman, for sale. We used to get the abalone and we used to cook it there on the rocks. In a kerosene tin, get four or five kerosene tins, we used to boil them there and dry them on the rocks . . . and they'd go as hard as a board. And he used to take them to Sydney and sell them.

Sarah: I think he used to send them to China.

Ben: He used to send them to China. They used to soak them in water, soak them then they'd come soft.[7]

Mickey of Ulladulla's sketch of camp life shows women boiling up mutton fish and drying it out on sheets in the sun for the Chinese market as described by Ben and Ossie Cruse.

Ossie: In regards to gathering mutton fish for commercial purposes, my dad and my uncles used to do this way back in the early 1900s. They used to gather mutton fish and trade with Chinese people. They used to take the meat out of the shell and while they were doing this it would really be a family gathering, where men would be diving, gathering the mutton fish, bringing it to share and women and kids would be lighting the fires. And they'd have these big drums to put the mutton fish in. They'd boil it for about three or four minutes and this would take all the impurities off the outside of the mutton fish, and they would come out of the boiling water looking a nice golden brown. Then the mutton fish would be laid out on the rocks in the sun to dry . . . [turning them over every hour so as to season the flesh properly]

Now, the drying process took two to three days, according to how hot the weather was, this was mainly a summer industry because the sun was at its hottest and the rocks used to be hot too.

Mickey of Ulladulla's drawing of scenes of Aboriginal life.

> What happened then was that the dry shell fish was placed in the big corn bags that used to take about 5 drums of mutton fish dried out. Now to get 5 drums of mutton fish it would take about 12 or 14 drums because they used to shrink so much when they were dried. And then they would be sewed up and kept in a dry place, then weighed and sold to the Chinese . . . So our people started trading way back then.[8]

Some families made a living entirely from fishing and lived in permanent camps at good fishing spots, such as the Brierlys at the mouth of the Moruya River and the Nyes at Barling's Beach near Tomakin. Others combined this with the seasonal farm work, especially when the intensive production of beans, peas and corn began in the 1930s. Beach camps could be found close to the beanfields, providing fresh food for the off season times. Paul Hudson grew up in the 1950s and describes the seasonal life:

> **Paul:** We used to live at Nerrigundah, and we'd pick beans for three to four months of year and after we'd finished the seasonal

Mutton Fish

Cleaning mutton fish on the rocks at Eden, 1995.

work we'd go down to Potato Point by the ocean and camp, we used to camp for about four to six months at a time and all we did was fish and just live off the ocean mainly, gathering mutton fish all the time. That was a sort of everyday thing for food, fishing and that. Just done that for about thirty years, thirty-five years all of our family, plus there was a lot of other families that used to do exactly the same as us. You know there were hundreds of people that used to do the seasonal work and camp and do the same as we did.

Liddy: Do you remember how you used to get them [mutton fish]? Because they used to be plentiful in those days.

Paul: Oh yeah, like they'd be in feeding at low tide, but like today you'd have to wait until low tide to pick them up but they were just lousy years ago, you could just pick them up on the rocks everywhere, they were just plentiful, they were everywhere. We just got them off the rocks and rubbed them on the rocks and got a rock and tenderised them and took them back to the camp with us and put them into the open fire or in the shell and grilled them.[9]

Life on the Beaches

Experience of life on the beaches carried on up to the 1970s and still today Koori people on the south coast teach their children the survival skills they learnt from the older generations. In researching *Mutton Fish* we interviewed more than twenty people about their experiences of growing up on the south coast and these interviews form the basis for this section of the book.[1]

Dorrie Stewart, whose father, Jimmy Chapman was a mill worker, grew up in the 1920s and was one of the children to benefit from the action of Jane Duren and others to preserve the land in Bateman's Bay. Living in the town didn't prevent these families from making full use of the sea's resources. This supplemented the basic rations they collected from local police in the time of the Depression. Dorrie remembers these times as a child with free access to beaches around the Bay:

> **Dorrie**: Years ago we had a sulky and van. Poor old Grandfather and Dad, he had a horse and sulky and van, cart. We used to walk then, all us kids, we used to walk behind the van or cart, got all the gear on it. No tents in them days, just blankets round like mia mias. This was all dirt road down there then, no road then, just dirt roads. Went to the beach, that's all we'd live on. Aunty Rita and Grandma Chapman used to take flour and sugar and tea, that's the main things. And we'd make the damper on the rocks and just cook it in the ashes. Mix 'em up on the rock with the salt water, seawater, that'd put the salt in it.

Beryl: Mix it up with the salt water, the damper, you didn't have a pot or anything, you'd mix it on the rocks?

Dorrie: Yes, knead it on the rocks and spread it out and then take it and put it in the hot ashes.

Beryl: Never heard of that one before.

Liddy: What about the mutton fish, did you used to get mutton fish then?

Dorrie: Yeah, you could get mutton fish, you could get anything out of the sea then. You didn't have to dive for it, it was round the edges you'd just get down with a knife or file and get it out. Just pull them off. In those days we'd just get a feed, wouldn't take the lot.

Beryl: But your rations would be just your milk and your tea.

Dorrie: We all had little bags, taking them up, getting them filled: flour, sugar, tea, rice. You'd get meat and bread, once or twice a week I think. Every Thursday we were rationed I think.

Beryl: But the meat wouldn't last long, because then they'd end up on the beach looking for fish and oyster and things like that, mutton fish.

Dorrie: In them days they didn't have fridges or nothing to keep anything, see. What they got they ate today and then go out and get the second lot. No keeping things for weeks and weeks and weeks. It was good in those days, they'd get out and go and hunt for rabbit, or anything. Oh, Aunty Rita she was out there if she wanted porcupine, she'd bake it up nice in the camp oven. We'd just get enough to eat and that was all, go back the next day, that's what we used to do, we didn't get a lot of stuff to go to waste. That would be no good. Old people wouldn't let us. They wouldn't let the kids waste them, no way. Everything out of the sea, they didn't waste nothing. And they didn't go and get bags and bags like they do today.

Liddy Stewart, Dorrie Stewart and Beryl Cruse, Bateman's Bay, 1997.

Beryl: That was the thing with the Kooris. They'd go down the beach and they'd have their feed. Have a game with the kids and they'd end up with a card game.

Dorrie: I'll never forget that, they still do that. That was their ways. I'll never forget going down there at Batehaven. Oh, big game on there now. Big card games. Break out this big pot on the fireplace, pot with a tin of stew in it to cook dinner in it. And I never used to play cards then, just standing watching them play. Anyhow, next thing there's BOOM everything goes off. Went dry and it had the lid on. Had it all in the tent. BOOM, the pot went up and the tin went up and the kids was flying everywhere.[2]

Jean Squires, now in her sixties, worked all her life fishing. At a young age she lived with her grandparents, the Brierlys, and learnt from them. They continued a tradition of commercial fishing learnt from their family's first contact with white culture in the 1840s at the whaling station in Twofold Bay. They were based on the Moruya River at Garland Town near the Moruya airport and Jean hauled nets from a young age. Later she raised her own family while continuing to fish for a living.

> **Jean**: We had a home at Broulee at one stage, right on Candlegut Beach there, you had to walk over the sandhills and be on the beach. Margaret was only a baby and the other kids were only all little steps and stairs. I'd be up and gone, three or four o'clock in the morning, I'd just leave them in their beds, and I'd go home every ten minutes to check on them. And that went on for years. We'd have the fish-shot in and up the beach before Brierlys got there. All they had to do was load them on the truck and take them. But I used to check on the kids, soon ever they woke up I'd feed them their breakfast and take them all over the beach with me. When they were babies I'd dig a little hole in the sand, put the blanket in it and lay them in there. And many a time I dragged a big cane pram with two of the babies in it along the Bingie there, just fishing in the night-time for salmon. Hand lining. When it was too rough to fish, I always had the hand-line, I had a kid on my back, another one in my arms, [laughs] going along the beaches.
>
> **Beryl**: You would have lived on fish then?
>
> **Jean**: Yes, and abalone and lobsters. When we were out on the beach just on daylight you'd shoot for mullet. Fire going and just throw them on to the coals. Everyone had their own no matter what crew it was they used to take fish out of the first batch they shot. And you'd be eating mullet at six o'clock in the morning, just throw them onto the coals. And the billycan was never off the boil; it was boiling the whole time you'd have your fire going. We used to go to Moruya. I'd pack the kids up at 2 o'clock in the morning, put them in the car, blankets and everything and take them out to the beach for the mullet; I had six or seven of them then. Weekends we'd go out and camp out there save getting the kids out of bed so early, that was our life. That's all we did.

Jean Squires,
Camden, 1997.

Beryl: That was the main food then, fried scones and fish and abalone and lobster.

Jean: But you used to make up a feed out of nothing in those days, out of nothing. Yes, you could always make a feed. All we seem to do is buy meat and that now. I used to do it for everyone. Go out to the beach with the Brierlys, they used to have tea. But I used to make fried scones at the beach too; we made a feed for everyone.

Beryl: Did you used to dive for abalone too?

Jean: I went into the suit once; I got into the suit once and went out and come in with a bag. But the suit was too hard to get in and out of. [laughter] Went down in the water, it was so pretty down under there, the fish and the rocks, all different colours.

Beryl: There probably were other women but I don't know of any other used to dive. I know they used to help clean abs and that.

Jean: My grandmother used to do a lot of fishing. I think that's where I got it from; they used to think she was a man. Used to be out at night hauling in the rivers and that with poor old Pardi. She used to be always fishing they used to just think she was another man. I was that way in the finish, I was just classed as another man. Men still used to swear up real big in front of me. It used to just go over my head. I wanted to be a fisherman, I wanted to be amongst men I had to hear all that.

Sue: How did you cook the abalone?

Jean: Take the black off, batter them down with a bottle or something, and then just roll them in flour and cook them. Make an onion gravy to go with it. And we used to mince them up, make patties out of them. It was so easy to go on the rocks in them days. It used to be so lovely walk around on the rocks. You didn't have to wet your feet to get the abalone in those days.[3]

Jean's son David remembers the times spent camping around the different beaches and how they lived on Broulee Island.

David: Yes, we lived there for three years. On the north west side, you come around this side of the island, and if you go up into the corner, into those big prickly things you should see all our names still there because we carved them into the big cactuses. Well we lived there.

Beryl: We had fresh water there too, didn't we, somewhere. I can't remember where.

David: Used to be springs, most of the places we lived we used to live near springs. I remember Broulee Island had a spring. Used to just leave a bucket out over night or through the day. You'd get a few buckets a day out of it, beautiful the water too.

Life on the Beaches

Sue: Did you eat much mutton fish when you were camping on the beaches?

David: That's what we survived on; fish, abalone, prawns . . . any seafood, anything a fisherman caught. That's what we say we always thought we had nothing but we ate better than anyone.

Liddy: Luxury today.

David: But you've got to think that a lot of months we didn't eat that either. We had to scrounge, go to chase rabbits or too rough to get in. Dad, he used to go away, we'd never seen him for months at times. Mum would go out with the fish on the fishing line, catch us tea. Maybe half a dozen bream, a couple of flathead. Go over them flats there at Moruya Heads, walk right across the flats in them big holes.

Sue: What was the camp like then, what did you have in the camp?

David: One big army tent and an outside fire. The one on the island wasn't bad because it had a sort of an overhang where you ate. And just a tin shed sort of put up with no walls in it, just a big table in the middle. I think there were seven of us, seven children and two grown ups. I just took to water. Even Billy used to say to me, 'You'd get a bloody lobster out of a bathtub.' But then I never drank or smoked then either, all I used to do was run, chase a football, I was chasing a football career. I used to run four miles every morning and every afternoon. Then I used to go chasing rabbits with the boys, Georgie Parsons and Frankie and all those. Used to get fifteen miles away from home and no walking, you run nearly all the way. Might stop at a sawmill on the way to grab a couple of those big square sticks they used to put out. Remember those big square sticks, about six foot long? Used to pole vault everything, never went through fences or anything, used to pole vault over them. That's what I mean, would have been in the Olympics with what we could do Yes, me and Jimmy at school, we never got beat in our cross-countries.

And the teachers used to go crook, 'What are you doing taking your shoes off?' 'Oh, we can't run in shoes.'

Beryl: Old fisherman.

David: It wasn't that, we never ever wore them. Like five o'clock in the morning, out in the heaviest bloody big dew. It used to be ice at Moruya. Used to be this high the grass and we used to slip in it, go out in the morning, five o'clock in the morning and slide all through it in a T shirt. Never felt the cold, run through blackberries, no worries.

Liddy: Today, do that today, you'd be in a lot of strife.

David: My feet would fall off if I didn't put me thongs on or me shoes. But in them days, I can remember Mum breaking lots and lots of needles trying to get the blackberry prickles out of our feet. Just bend them and break them.

Liddy: Real wiry lad.

David: Ah, but that's all we ever done see, we used to get up of a morning go down and see George and them, they used to live down the bottom. We were in the old house but they used to live down in the bush down near the bull paddock. They used to only live in water tanks. One had the whole lot just turned up side down with a doorway cut in it. Their mum and them used to sleep in a half a one. And we used to go fishing and go to school chase rabbits with them. They taught us lots.

Beryl: But even when you lived in town your father still fished?

David: Yeah, me father fished ever since I can remember. He got tipped over on the bar, him and my uncle George, they had a twenty-two footer, and he had to swim two miles. Because the seas were that big he had to swim up the river and come right into that little lagoon. And all he was worried about, even being in the water all the time, all he was worried about was that the sea had ripped all his clothes off and he wouldn't get out of the water.[4]

Life on the Beaches

Ronnie Nye grew up on the beaches around Moruya and was taught diving by his uncles:

Ronnie: Dad and Uncle Andy, used to get around, they never had goggles and those things in their day . . . Yes, with their clothes on they used to walk around the rocks and stick their feet in the holes all that there. And they'd come back to the camp at Barling's with cornbags full. Lobsters and mutton fish, they'd have a cornbag, one on each shoulder, bringing back from round the rocks. I remember David telling me there one day that Uncle Andy went around there, Uncle Andy Nye, and he caught that many lobsters that he sunk the boat. He had the boat chock a block full and sunk it, 12 foot fishing boat, sunk it, yeah. You didn't have to go that far to get a few.

Liddy: When your uncle came back with the bag full that was to feed all the family?

Ronnie: Yes, feed all the family, even me father-in-law used to tell before he died, Henry Chapman, he was telling me about when he used to go down here on the pushbike. He used to get that many lobsters and mutton fish he used to sell them. For bread and stuff like that, the old barter system.

Beryl: Because they knew just exactly where to go too.

Ronnie: Yes, that's right. They had a hole out at Barling's Island there. And they used to carry a big rock out to Barling's and use it to jump over the side, to take them down. And grab the lobsters out of the hole, right down the bottom. They used to take a smally [hipflask] with them in the wintertime.

Beryl: They'd have all their old clothes on?

Ronnie: Yeah, the jumpers on yeah. Everything I've been taught has come through the family, it's been handed down right through. It just comes natural and from when you were a kid and you'd come up to the age of the goggles and snorkel. When you're going to school and you'd come home on the weekends and the elder boys like Andrew and them and they were going out doing it. And you turn around and you'd just say, right give us a go at it. You start to learn to use a snorkel and goggles and flippers and you're into it straight away.[5]

Tina Mongta grew up on the far south coast in the early 1950s. Her parents, Wally and Natalie Mongta, lived on the resources of the sea, and the children were taught the self-sufficiency needed to survive. It was often a hard lesson:

Sue: Where were your favourite spots for mutton fish around here?

Tina: Greencape was the main one. We used to camp all along there you know. Stay there a couple of weeks at all the different little spots around Disaster Bay. Then we'd go around to Wonboyn, back around. We were around there with the Holmes too. Remember the Holmes was camping out there for years and we used to all camp with them. Get the water out of the rocks and Dad would take a shovel and if there wasn't any water in the rocks where we was camping he'd dig a big sand hole, well back from the sea, and strain it. It used to just fill up and we'd grab the water out of the hole and just strain it and use it that way, boil it up. Then when it'd get cold have it that way.

Beryl: But it wasn't a day thing, you'd camp there?

Tina: Yes, camp there, fishing and diving whatever they used to do. And us kids have a good run, wild, in the bush. Wapengo was one of the main spots too. If we didn't do any fishing there, you could always get a feed of mussels and oysters, and bimbulas (Sydney cockles). Sit up all night fishing. We used to be made to sit up. Weren't allowed to go to sleep, he made us catch our own, feed ourselves. Just to teach us how to stay up. Take us down to the beaches and show us what to eat and what not to eat, and if we didn't listen, he'd pull the strap straight off, eh? Give us a hiding.

Tina: Down at the Kiah River he used to spear the biggest blue-nosed bream, real big lads like that. And take them into the

Tina Mongta, Eden, 2004.

shops in here, if we had no picking, take them in there and the bully mullets, they used to be the main one, and Dad would swap it for bread and milk, things like that. We went to school at Palestine [Creek, north of Eden], used to go down the rocks and get all the seafood we can, get all the penny winkles, abalone, and fishing. Get oysters and mussels there then.

Liddy: So you've had a go diving down for the mutton fish?

Tina: No, no I just walk around the rocks and get them off the rocks. Used to take them home for our parents because they used to go picking sometimes, and older ones, us, used to just watch the little ones, take them for walks. Take a line with us. That's going back into the late fifties, early sixties.

Sue: That was before anyone else was fishing mutton fish.

Tina: Yes, no-one used to take it then.

Sue: What other bush tucker, you were saying you had to feed yourself?

Tina: Oh, I remember we had a big swan. We had nothing else except Dad had to shoot a swan for Christmas dinner to give us.

Wally Mongta, Tina's father in Eden, 1991.

That was camping on this side of Wallaga Lake before we moved over on the mission . . . over near Uncle Tom's cabin in the bush there. They had a big bus there and we used to camp in that bus. And we had nothing this Christmas, and Dad said ,'Well, the kids are not going to go without, we gotta eat.' So he went a shot a couple of swans and done them up.

Liddy: Were they nice?

Tina: No we didn't like them. We had to eat them, eat or get the strap. There were swans, there were duck eggs. Used to go collecting duck eggs. There was a lot of rabbits, we used to eat heaps of rabbits but there were no diseases in those days, it was good. There was a heap of bush tucker we used to eat; geebungs, wild cherries, wondarmas [apple berries], he showed us all that. Porcupine, we've had that, never ate a goanna or a snake. He give us a taste of, what do you call them things, witchetty grubs and we wouldn't eat them.[6]

Life on the Beaches

Mutton fish were plentiful on the reefs and could easily be picked up from around the water's edge. Ossie Stewart applied his creative mind to designing the ultimate mutton fish gathering tool from things he found around the place. Liddy tells the story:

> The year was about 1963. I was living with my family in a little house on a hill right near Camel Rock in Bermagui. I was married and Ossie and I had Alice who was going on for two years old. We were doing some seasonal work for a Mr Went and at this stage the work was very poor. It was a lovely spot where we were, close to the beach and the weather was great so when we weren't picking peas we would go fishing at Camel Rock or go down the road to the bridge over Wallaga Lake and fish in the lake. We would also get big mud oysters whenever we felt like them.
>
> My brothers and sisters were only young and they would follow Ossie when he went fishing. One day they went down to the beach and Ossie said he'd have a go at getting some mutton fish. He didn't have diving gear but he was going in to have a look. They were gone for quite a while and returned with a good feed of mutton fish. The kids were all excited about it and Ossie said he had seen a lot more mutton fish deep down in the crevices. He said, 'If I had something to reach them without even having to go into the water, I think I'll make something to get them out of the crevices.'
>
> Next day Ossie and the kids were busy getting things together to make this contraption and I remember them coming in to show me when the great work of art was finished. The kids were very proud of Ossie and what he'd done, and they were anxious to see it working. It was a long stick, a bit longer than a broomstick, and on one end were the sole of an old sand shoe and half of a tyre lever tied together with strips off a tyre tube. Connected to this was thin wire going up the stick to an old bike brake. When this was pressed down the sandshoe sole would lift up from the tyre lever that would be pushed under the mutton fish in the crevice. Then the brake would be let go and the sandshoe would clamp down on the mutton fish and hold it as the stick was pulled out.

Mutton Fish

Liddy Stewart holding a copy of the original mutton fish gathering tool made by her husband Ossie Stewart, 2003.

Well they couldn't wait until the tide went out to try it and when they did it was successful, it worked like a charm. People were quite surprised to see this man on the rocks with the kids pulling up big mutton fish with this strange contraption. So you can imagine we had some good meals there whenever we felt like mutton fish. I wonder what they would do if they used something like this today, although back in that time the mutton fish were very plentiful around the rocks and only the Kooris knew how good they were to eat.

Like the traditional people described in chapter one, Koori people love to tell yarns of the day's events for the amusement of their audience. This poem, written by Liddy's uncle, Stanley Nean, continues this tradition. It is about her brother James and husband Ossie, and their attempt to pass on the skills of diving to the younger generation.

The Divers

'The young ones of today,' Jimmy casually said,
To old Oss as he poured out a beer.
'They don't seem to have the nous that we had
And their lives are so stagnant and drear.
They seem really thick; I'm just lost for words
How in God's name will they ever survive?
What say that we take them all out one day
And teach the young lads how to dive.

'They'll have to learn just what terror is,
And about all how to comprehend
When they come face to face with the dangers out there,
It'll sort out the boys from the men.'
And old Oss he hung onto Jim's every word
With a nod of his old knowing head.
'That's very true,' said he. 'I must really concur
James with every word that you said.'

Thus the plans were laid out for one free weekend
To be spent at the bay by the foam
There to pass all their knowledge onto each lad
All the skills and crafts that they'd known.
So there by the bay where golden sands gleam,
Their campsites were set upon the beach.
The diving art to be taught to every young lad
An open-air classroom so to speak.

The young lads gathered round, the first lessons began
The eagerness on each face was astute.
As the demonstration commenced by Oswald and Jimmy
Just how to don their first diving suit.
The tutor's suits were obtained some twelve years before
When their torsos were youthful and lean
But alas with the years came the middle-age spread
And fitting it in was a sight to be seen.

Mutton Fish

So in silence the lads looked on in amaze.
Their young faces and minds were agog
At the straining and groaning with wrestling the zips
And their eyes bulging out like a frog.
One from the crowd gathered there at the scene
Remarked, 'They looked like nothing on earth,'
As they walked in reverse to the edge of the shore
Then disappeared 'neath the waves of the surf.

Down through the shadows of a far different world
To the kelp-covered shelf of the reef
Gracefully they floated on over the edge
That falls away to the depths of the deep.
Down ever downward where the sunlight grows dim
And the shadows wax stronger and dark
Like dolphins they slipped o'er the last reef
And head on met the giant grey nurse shark.

Now the crowd that remained above in the shore
Were eagerly waiting the diver's return.
A lad called loudly, 'There's movement out there.'
As the bay's waters began to violently churn
And running on top of the waves there appeared
Two men in their tight diving suits
And close at their heels, was the large dorsal fin
Of the grey nurse shark in pursuit.

With inches to spare they both hit the shore
They made it just out of his reach
And passing on through the open-air school
They pulled up three miles down the beach
Diving suits were a mess all zippers were gone
Their middle-age spread was enjoying the breeze
The goggles were left somewhere in the deep
And their flippers were up round their knees.

A witness recalls the sight she had seen
She said, 'In my mind forever shall be
'Twas like turning the pages back two thousand years

When it was first done on the Galilee Sea.
But the Lord calmed the waters for men to survive
On that day when Heavens grew dark.
But these lads were saving their middle-age spread
From the jaws of that great grey nurse shark.'

Terribly shaken with fright and trembling with fear
With hair standing straight up on end
Their voices were ravelled when trying to speak
The poor lads were near round the bend.
When colour returned to their blizzard-like face
And at last the blood started to flow
The students were found at the edge of the shore
In diving gear and all ready to go.

The tutors regained their composure once more
Nerves of steel once again became cool
Then a decision was reached by Jimmy and Oss
They decided to close down the school.
When the young lads inquired what reason there was
Their queries were met with rebuff
The tutors' answers were simply, a blind man can see
Out there that the seas are too rough.

'Yes the young ones today,' Jimmy casually remarked,
to old Oss as he poured him a beer
'They don't seem to have the nerves that we had
and their lives are so timid and drear
They just seem so thick and I'm lost really for words
Of the chances in their lives that they miss.
What say that we take them all out for the day
And teach them all how to fish.'[7]

In the first chapter Sarah Colley described a midden deposit site at Disaster Bay, Wonboyn, going back about six hundred years. Beryl and Ossie Cruse camped there with their young family in the 1960s. They helped the Holmes family to beach-net salmon for the cannery in Eden. Their lifestyle of living from the beaches continued in the manner of the traditional people who left shells, bones and boot buttons in the caves behind the beach. The attractions of a sheltered camp site, rocky shelves for shellfish, a long open beach and cliffs for clear lookouts would have been valued by fishers at any time.

Sue: What was it like when you used to camp here?

Ossie: In those days it was a time when we had a lot of freedom, and we used to travel doing seasonal work or fish and camp wherever we wanted to camp. There were a lot of places to camp too. And I remember that we used to fish with a bloke called Billy Holmes at Broulee Beach up near Moruya. And he heard about the big catches of fish down here at Eden. So he moved down here and the first year that they were here they caught something like 14 ton of fish, from memory. We were only getting small catches up there, so we followed them down and after a while we came down here and we all camped down on the other end of that beach there; Greenglades.

Beryl: Yes, but remember we were coming back from seasonal work and we met Uncle Billy at the shop there at Kiah.

Ossie: Yes, that's right. Really carefree life, kids were only small and we used to dive along the rocks there. You'd get mutton fish and lobsters and then Basil Andy used to go over to that lake there at Merrica and spear these beautiful big bream. We were fishing for salmon mainly there then and it was a real delicacy to have a nice bream cooked up. Yes they were the times when we didn't have any ties because we didn't rent a house, we didn't have a house to look after. We didn't have any anchors and we used to travel just anywhere between Port Augusta and Bundaberg Queensland.

Sue: On that beach round there you had your camp set up, where did you get your water?

Ossie: We used to carry our water in. We used to bring it in either from the guesthouse or from the river. We used to go back up into the fresh water up here, the other side of Wonboyn

Dennis, Ossie and Beryl Cruse, 1970.

settlement. We went up there a few times 'cause that was the best place to wash, wasn't it? Take the washing up there. Course we didn't have a lot of clothes to wash in those days. We didn't want to carry a lot of stuff around when you only had the one old car. We used to pack everything in the old car when we had three kids. I think at that time I had an old grey Ford ute.

It's a pity that there isn't more places set aside like that for people to go and camp and get away from the stress of things. Society seems to be locking ourselves into a real stressful situation. You've got all these commitments, you've got to pay your rent and electricity and everything that comes with renting a house. We never had that because we could just pitch our tent anywhere. We didn't have incomes then because we never applied for social service. Even when we were fishing for one year to the other we used to just go and get the food off the rocks, you know lobsters, fish, mutton fish. Dennis when he was a little boy used to get these couple of fish and he'd go over, he'd gut them and clean them and he'd take them away and sell them to the tourists. How old was he, he was only little then eh? Little bloke, he'd go and barter with the tourists. Selling these fish and he'd come back with a pocket full of lollies, some delicacy that he couldn't have.

Sue: Those middens we saw, the caves. Did you know about them when you were there?

Ossie: We didn't know about those. Middens were everywhere in those days, you didn't treat them as anything special. Now that a lot of development, particularly a lot of foreshore development up the coast, there's not much of our cultural heritage left now. That's why all these things have become important.

Beryl: We didn't take notice of the middens.

Sue: Do you think your lifestyle would have been very different to how those people who made those middens would have lived?

Ossie: Well not really they were still the same carefree and nomads. You know they were people who would have followed the seasons same as we did.

Beryl: You'd eat the food off the land and sea and that.

Ossie: And we used to, even with Dad when I was growing up we used to follow the seasons. And one of the seasons we used to follow was the westerly season for the mutton fish. Dad and I, and all of us as a family, would go out on the rocks, especially when the westerly wind would come — seas nice and calm, and the kids would all be picking the mutton fish off the rocks. We'd have these big drums and we'd cure them and then we'd take it in turns turning them and we'd dry them in the sun. And they used to dry a nice golden brown. And we'd have these dried bags, big potato bags, clean; we'd washed them to make them clean. And we'd fill them up; sometimes we'd get six to eight bags, dried like that. We were getting eight pound a bag; we sold 'em to the Chinese. Because Dad was reared with Chinese, he knew that they used to love, mutton fish. They used to sell them to China. We were really the forerunners of this abalone industry, because we used to sell them, used to make a lot of money, as far as money was concerned in those days.

Eight pound was a lot of money for a family to have in those days. We used to get eight, ten times over.

The cultural lifestyle would have been like that, for Kooris, up to the early seventies. And it was the early seventies when they were starting to get houses, you know. They were starting to be allocated houses in towns, and that's when the whole lifestyle changes. And that's when, besides, the machinery came in too and took over the harvesting of the various crops we used to pick by hand. Peas and beans, even tomatoes and grapes, they've even got machines that will pick grapes. But a lot of them have gone back to hand picking now, those machines didn't really work out. But they were the big seasons. It would be nothing for you to go to a place like Bairnsdale, Bega or Bodalla and you'd find three to six hundred Kooris just coming for the picking in the bean paddock. And they were good days when people used to share, share a lot. If they knew that someone didn't have anything you'd share what you had with people.

Beryl: But you'd see everyone nearly everyday though wouldn't you?

Ossie: Wasn't a lot of drink in those days. Sometimes on weekends, a few of the old mates like. But most people used to enjoy themselves a lot. It was good, good lifestyle, but as soon as we got into houses we sort of locked the door . . . [8]

Abalone

Put in for a licence

Round about the late 50's, early 60's was when the western world started to get knowledge of abalone. And it was in the mid- 60's that the industry started to kick off in New South Wales. It first started in the Gulf of Mexico and up along the west coast of America, California. White people out here used to laugh at the Koories when they used to be gathering mutton fish, they used to accuse them of eating snails. But when they started to taste the beautiful flavour of mutton fish it became a known delicacy in Australia. But particularly they found out that the Asian world used to thrive on mutton fish. So that, when it became popular, the name then became known as abalone.

We ourselves, Aboriginal people started to capitalise on the market for abalone and a lot of our traditional way of preserving abalone was taken away because that was free-for-all then because everybody started diving. Even kids after school used to dive. And everybody on the south coast was involved in it in some shape or form; at least there were hundreds of divers that were involved in diving for abalone and selling it to these markets that opened up.[1] (Ossie Cruse).

Big changes in the lives and livelihood of the Koories of the south coast came in the 1960s. The 1967 referendum brought citizenship rights, and coalitions of white and black activists pushed for land and housing. On the south coast the Koories started to settle in towns. This meant they were no longer reliant on the farmers and were released from the need to work in the fields in return for a place to live.

Abalone

The opportunity to make good money using skills practised from an early age presented itself when the commercial market for abalone opened up. Suddenly the Koori's long-ignored subsistence food, the humble mutton fish, was in demand and lives changed as divers came from all over Australia and New Zealand to grab what they could.

BJ Cruse started diving for abalone at ten or eleven years of age, but began diving at seven, 'When I was seven, we used to dive off the wharves at Larpa. Tourists used to chuck money in, coins, for the black kids.' He recalls how his father made their own goggles to get into the abalone rush.

> **BJ**: I remember Dad making a pair of goggles. He made them out of a tyre tube, and cracked a windowpane with a piece of wet clay and hot water. Made a glass and then cut the tube with the straps on it and stuck it all together and tied it on and that's what he did. I know we used to do a lot of diving, a lot of gathering of fish, shellfish and so forth. I remember in about 1967 when Dad was diving at Mystery Bay. I think it was about 12 divers in the diving crew, including Uncle Merv Penrith, Uncle Basil Andy, Jimmy Pender, Dad, Brian Mongta, Dennis and a few of the young fellas sort of come and went. We actually harvested abalone, and basically nothing else, except for food. Maybe some lobsters or whatever. Before that we harvested seafood but I'm not sure whether it was abalone or not, it probably was. It's only because we was in it as an industry that I remember specifically diving for abalone.
>
> In '67 they was getting nineteen cents a pound. And there was that many abs around that Dad used to knock off by two o'clock. And by two o'clock he'd have eight big round garbage bins of abalone meat. And we'd have to have them shelled, and we had a FJ ute with a canvas in the back, and we used to spill them straight in on the canvas. We'd have nearly half a ute full of abalone meat see, but we were only getting about 19 cents a pound.
>
> **Sue**: And what did you do with that abalone?
>
> **BJ**: Well, they were sold. I think we first started selling them through a, not a co-op, but through a person who was sort of

doing a contract-sale thing I guess. We used to sell them to a bloke at Bermagui by the name of Gordon Beaver. He had a little place at the back of his house where you weighed them in, and then he organised to bring them through to Eden. And I think there was Owen Allen and there's Gordon Lucas. Now one of those two come first, I'm not sure which one it was. That was 1967. And then SAFCOL come later. They come around, leading up to when licences become saleable.

Liddy: How long did your father do that for, until the licences were introduced?

BJ: Well, basically Dad dove there '67. Dad could've come down earlier when I was younger, I can't remember. We went from 1967; I think the mission managers were just moving, ready to move off the mission about that time. That place called Mystery Bay, we give them places names, they've still got them today. And not a lot of people know them. The paddock where we used to camp, we camped in the scrub, in the tree line and there was a paddock to the south a bit. When we set up the camp, Dad sent the kids down to get some water, and we come down and we seen this sign on the post, 1080 poison. So, we went back up and said, 'You can't drink the water down there because it's 1080 poisoning.' So they call that place 1080 now, 1080 paddock, you see. And there was another place that, a handkerchief lake south of Narooma, we used to drive the car in there, and we used to carry the air compressor, Dad used to carry that. Me and Dennis used to lift it on his shoulders, because it was heavy. And he used to walk from there to Glasshouse. And that's quite a few kilometres, probably about four or five kilometres, he used to carry this thing, and we had to be there by the time he got there to lift it off his shoulders. We call that place Long Carry. And some people they hear the name and they think you're talking about a shell. That's where that got its name from. There's a few other places with names too.

David Squires grew up in a fishing family near Moruya. His mother, Jean, grew up fishing with her grandfather Walter Brierly, also known as Pardi, and was still fishing with her son Ernie into her sixties. David didn't stay in fishing, 'Because I wasn't a fisherman, I never wanted to be a fisherman in my whole life.' He now works as the Aboriginal Education Assistant at Eden Public School, acting on his passion to help children achieve their full potential. In the 1960s he worked in Eden in the early commercial abalone fishery.

> **David**: I went to school up till fifteen, about '66 I think I left it then, '65 or '66. I might have been only fourteen because I wanted to keep going, and they said, 'No, there's too many kids, you've got to help raise them.' And we camped down at Merimbula, just me and me father and I was sixteen years old. It was in the middle of winter and we were potting for lobsters. We come down and sold some lobsters and we heard people talking about abs, and he said to me, 'What do you reckon, we've got enough money to buy a pair of goggles, what do you reckon, we have a go?' And I said, 'Yeah, okay.' So I went in, in a T-shirt, pair of shorts in the middle of winter and a pair of shoes, started diving. Dived like that for nine days, and when we come down and sold the abs, I went and asked the bloke we sold them to

David Squires, Eden Public School, 2004.

would he go guarantor for a suit and Dad got one and I got one. He started diving then, he was too old to dive with no suit on. We dived around Merimbula for a while, then we went back up to Moruya and I think we built the house. No, no we never built the house until after a couple of years diving. We was at Minora still, we must have been still living in the old house.

Beryl: The one who went guarantor for a suit. Did you and your father get a diving thing, you know that you used to carry around?

David: Little compressor? Owen Allen went guarantor for that and a boat, after we'd dived for him for a few months, yeah.

Beryl: Well that's how Ossie got his compressor [the Scuba Boy] too, after your father got his. And we used to carry it around the rocks.

David: Well they only weighed seventy pound or something didn't it? And it used to pump two people, used to float around on a big tube and the compressor was in the middle. And turn it up side down and you only had twenty-five foot of hose; and two blokes trying to go one way each. That was hard (laughter). Used to end up pulling over, but it never ever stopped, like it would stop and you just give it one pull and she'd start up again.

Liddy: What about the mutton fish, there would have been plenty then?

David: Well me and my brother Ernie when we started diving with the air, we used to pull two and a half ton a week. We never ever seen any money, we used to see ten dollars a week of it. I don't know, what was your wages; I come down here and worked when I was eighteen, and it was only $33.30 for forty hours. But I think we were pulling usually around $1250 a week. Like when we first started I think wages were only $21 or something. And we built that four-bedroom house.

Beryl: Your mother went out in the boat, cleaned abalone and that too?

David: Yeah, Mum used to come in the boat with us all the time. She's a good sheller too, she could shell. She could shuck all right. Dad would be there but he just used to keep an eye on it, make sure there were no sharks or anything coming around. Mum would take abs from us where we come out of the water and clean them and he'd be sitting up on the hill over there making sure there was nothing dangerous around. Like, you know, they used to make sure you were safe.

Liddy: And where would you sell it in those days?

David: We used to sell to Owen Allen. And any lobsters we got we used to sell to Cookie at Bateman's Bay. That's where we use to sell all our crayfish. But we dived, what from right up past Durras right down to Eden, all the way down, Bermagui, everywhere.[2]

The buying of abalone became more competitive as the price went up in the 1970s seventies. BJ Cruse and his brother Dennis took it in their own hands to stay in the business on their own terms.

BJ: We were diving for Owen Allen and Gordon Beaver in '67. Later on when we moved we sold directly through Owen Allen, then he went out of business and later on Gordon Lucas started buying abalone, and we sold to Gordon Lucas right up to not long before licences were issued, then he went out of business too. And one day we come in with 12 bins of abalone in the back of a FB station wagon see. And we went down to Lucas and he said, 'No,' he said, 'I don't buy them no more.' We didn't even know. So we went across the road to SAFCOL and we said, 'We got some abs we want to get rid of them.' And they said, 'We can't buy them because you're not a member of the association.' We said, 'What association?' Apparently there was an association. Anyway he refused to buy our abalone. So we said, 'We're going to be selling our abalone on the fish market in Sydney, and we're going to be selling them to the highest bidder and we're going to have, I'm not sure whether it's a Current Affair, and we challenge you to come down and book us.' And that's what we did. And we went to Sydney and we got a good price for our abs too. Chinamen pushing each other out of the road, and Dennis only pulled one bin out at a time too. Made them bid and they all bidded. No one stopped us, we had twelve bins of abs spread out, just back up to some big shed up there and spread them out on the floor. Then SAFCOL rang us up and said it was all right to buy our abalone, and I think licences were issued after that.

Sue: And they never offered for you to become members of the association?

BJ: They could have, but we didn't see no need. We were always self employed and we always were our own managers of our lives, we never saw a need for a association, particularly when we knew we were in the business before they even knew what association meant.

The licences were bought in to restrict access to the NSW abalone fishery, which had grown from 18 tonnes in 1964–65 to a peak of 1,200 tonnes in 1971. In 1977, catches fell to 300 tonnes due to

BJ in his diving gear, 1983.

heavy fishing and damage from severe storms and it was recommended by a Parliamentary Select Committee of Inquiry that the abalone and sea urchin become a limited entry fishery. Although they had been diving for many years most of the Koories missed out on getting licences as they hadn't worked as consistently as other more organised and better-capitalised divers. The restricted permit introduced in 1980 required that, to qualify, divers had to show returns for an average catch of about 200 kg a month for at least six months each year over three years. They also had to prove, through tax records, that 51% of their income was from abalone. Only 59 divers were granted licences and the catch remained steady at about 600 tonnes a year.[3]

> **Sue**: So when you were diving for abs did you get a licence when the licences came in? Were you still diving when that happened?
>
> **David**: No, I never put in for a licence; which were silly, I should have. They reckoned we couldn't get a licence because we had no records of what we got. You see Ernie [David's brother] kept all his records but the old man never did. Then of the people that started it I reckon only 5% got licences. All the rest were people that had money and come into it. And they're the ones that changed it.

BJ Cruse describes the introduction of the licences:

> **BJ**: First of all there was no such thing as a licence. What you had was a fishing licence, and then on the fishing licence they allowed you to collect abalone, and then later on they actually changed that licence and they stamped it, with permission to gather abalone, turban shells and sea eggs [sea urchins]. That's on an abalone licence. Then later on they actually took it off the fishing licence, it was a permit, under a fishing licence, they took it off that and made it a licence in it's own right, sort of thing.

Although diving paid good money, (in 1979 it was recommended that $26,000 was a reasonable rate,)[4] professional diving for abalone is hard and dangerous work. BJ Cruse describes the daily toil and the competitive aspects of abalone industry:

Put in for a Licence

BJ's abalone diving logbook.

BJ: So it's like a desirable sort of thing that people want to do. It's like a fantasy, they get the picture of swimming around in this clear water with all the fish and that, but it's not like that see. You've got to get on the boat some mornings in the middle of winter. You'd get up about two or three o'clock in the morning and you'd leave Eden, and you'd drive up to Mystery Bay. It might be drizzling rain and a cold south-westerly wind blowing off the ice caps, and you wait until the sun rises long enough and you look down the black cold water and you got to put your wet diving suit on . . .

Liddy: So it's not as glamorous as people think it is!

BJ: No, (laughs) and see there's two different kinds of suit. There's a dry suit where you have warm clothes underneath and then there is a wet suit, and the way a wet suit works is that it only allows enough water in and it keeps that in there and it warms up to your body temperature. We had a tailor-made one so that the water didn't wash in and out. But the problem with wet suits is that takes over half an hour to get warm, and so for that first half an hour you feel every cold trickle, and that's when you work the hardest. When you first hit that water I remember you used to swim down the bottom and rip into it flat-out trying to warm up and when you get home at the end of the day, you're burning when you get up onto the deck with the cold salt air. You got to keep going, it was hard work.

BJ Cruse describes how he and his brother made a big catch of abalone in one day:

BJ: Me and Dennis, when abalone started to thin out, not long before we finished diving, we broke the record for the biggest catch of abalone in NSW. About 27 bins in one day.

Sue: Where was that?

BJ: That was at Bunga. You see Dennis knew the coast, he had an advantage. He could go down here and he could look at the two points on the southern side and on the north side and see which way the sea's coming from. Then he'd go down and look at the boat ramp and get an idea by the wash up and down the ramp how big the waves were. And then if he knew there was a certain wind that would blow up that would make a certain place perfect for diving. Then we always had the jump.
    That was the thing about abalone. Where you made your money was the rough seas, because it put everyone out of the water. For the first couple of weeks after the rough seas, probably a week or two weeks, then everywhere was packed. So what you've got to do is get to all the best places first. You've got to know when to take off. So when we broke the record he was watching this place for about six months, and without even leaving Eden knew that no one was diving there.
    So we left here about, two o'clock in the morning, and we sat on the side of the boat and waited for the sun to come up, see. And it was still dark when we jumped in the water and we just worked flat out all day, without getting out of the water, until it was too dark to see again. We'd just swim back to the bottom of the boat and then send the abs up on a rope and another bag would be there waiting for us.

Sue: So who was helping you when you were doing this?

BJ: We had a number of deckies, mostly all the mob. Peter Button might have been a deckie at that time. And then when we caught those abs, that's another time the ab diver's association convened this meeting, for us to answer against buying off poachers. And it was, I don't know his name, but his nickname, Fewsie. Fewsie used to live up the lighthouse there, up that way, big fella. Fewsie was there and he said, 'No the Cruse boys was there before I got there and they was still there when I left.' He said, 'No one seen them all day.' We never got out of the water all day.

The danger for long-term divers was the effect the sea pressure had on their ears, lungs and bones. There were procedures of decompression when coming up from a deep dive to help protect the diver, but in those early days the competition was intense and divers cut corners in their safety to maximise their catch. As the resource became depleted divers went deeper to find the abalone. BJ describes diving into the deep water off the coast, going down about 85 feet:

BJ: I dove out here, out from Boyd Tower, I went out as far as the hose could reach, out to what they call a sand line and that's when you start off in the water and you got your kelp line and you down a bit and there's a bit of granite rock and lots of sea eggs and you going out further and its like big canyons, big bombies just like cliffs. And you go down there and then there's all these real little boulders there, they all look the same, like river boulders, and they got moss all over them and sand mixed with them. And that's what they call a sand line, because out there is sand then, and it goes out toward the shelf. That's where the sharks are, I been out there a couple of times.

Both BJ and his brother Dennis had to leave the industry early due to medical problems:

BJ: Well he was the same with me. We were retired diving because of long-term exposure to those elements. I got a doctor's certificate, I actually got ordered out of the water by the doctors. Because of my health condition, see.

I was in about 75 foot of water and I had an accident. I had a lot of pain in the head, I was burning up and I had to get out of the suit cooling myself down. And then I had a couple of dives after that in about 18 foot of water and the same thing happened. I went to the doctors in Canberra and then they sent me to North Shore to the Naval Frogman Dive Centre. All these specialist doctors to the diving industry they run tests on my bones, blood and my sinuses. And what happen was my ears seized up you see, because me and Dennis was known by the white fellas as white-water divers, because we used to dive in the white water. And a lot of the reason why the whitefellas didn't like the white water was because there were too many wobbegongs there. I counted up to 48 wobbegongs in one day, in the one area. Too many wobbegongs because they came to feed on the lobsters in the weeds, and also in the white water it's too hard to work.

Sue: You're getting knocked around too much?

BJ: Yeah, because we did our training with the snorkelling, you see, we didn't really buy a boat. We were driving around in that blue FB station wagon there. That was around from the mid-sixties to the mid- seventies, ten years we did snorkel diving and we got used to diving in the currents. And when you get used to it you get the sea to work for you. So all you learn is to swim around in a straight line and you get to tell how big the waves are and when you need to go out or when you need to hang on and if you're going to get hurt and that's all like walking round. It's just like a part of life after a while, and you learn how to just swim along and the currents wash up and down and you pick the abs up you see.

See, problems occur when people go down and come up too fast. What happened with my problem was if you're diving in ten foot of water and you have a three- foot swell, that is waves are three foot high, and every wave the pressure is rising and dropping you see. And over those years all my sinuses seized up and my equalisers, because they were over worked. You see, it wasn't an accident from not knowing what to do, it was just being exposed to those things too long and too young, the same as the pimples on my bones on my hips. Those are pimples that occurred because I was exposed to that pressure before my bones matured you see, so by the time I was twenty-nine I was retired from diving. So basically from about '67 to '83, that's it.[5]

This was just before the price of abalone increased dramatically due to a sudden growth in international demand and the devaluation of the Australian dollar.

Carol Cruse, BJ's wife, first tasted abalone at the age of fourteen. She came to the south coast from Newcastle with her family to work in the bean paddocks and married BJ in 1978.

Carol: He and Dennis got into the diving then, he bought a truck and Dennis bought the boat, a shark cat. I remember in the rough weather we used to have to go [bean] picking. You didn't have full time diving because it was too rough. Most the time if it was too rough we used to go snorkelling, him and me would go snorkelling.

Sue: You'd get abalone and lobster?

On board the shark cat *Top Cat* in Eden, 1980s.

Carol: You'd get both around the rocks. If it was rough we do picking because you couldn't get a full-time job because if the weather was calm you'd just go to work.

Sue: When you had Serina as a little toddler and you'd go snorkelling, what did that mean? Did you take Serina down on the rocks?

Carol: Yeah, we used to take her or sometimes just leave her home with Mum, depends how cold or windy it was. We used to just sit her in the fish bin, me and her used to just sit on the rocks, take a big blanket.

Sue: Did you have to shell the abalone when they come up?

Carol: No they used to sell them in the shell, we weren't allowed to take them out of the shell. And take them down to get them weighed at the wharf. When him and Dennis got the truck and got into it they used to go in the early hours of the morning. Dennis would watch the news of a night and they'd get up in the dark and they'd get home in the dark. They'd have to wash all his gear and that. I think sometimes we used to take the hookah gear too on the rocks.

Sue: Did you used to worry?

Carol: No not really because I knew he was a diver. I used to go around with him and I knew he could dive so I didn't worry about things like that. Except when we had that big storm. A lot of them couldn't get in it was too rough. So me and Rhonda, we were worried so we went down looking for them. But we couldn't get down the wharf because all the sheds and that were all knocked down. So we was just sitting around over on the side waiting for them. They didn't get home till late but they had to go right around to Quarantine they got in that way. Yeah, that was a worry because it was wild the wind. BJ said the waves were just real big waves coming over like mountains.

Sue: You were saying you ate a lot of abalone and lobster in that time?

Put in for a Licence

Carol: Yeah, he'd sell them and some he'd give to the family, the old people.

Sue: Any favourite recipes?

Carol: No I just like them, just cook them, just fry them. My sister's kids used to come down too so we used to have to make rice and curries and gravies and stuff to go around. So we used to just make big pots of curry and rice. We used to mince it up and make a meatloaf, and bake it. Used to make the rissoles for Dad because Dad never had any teeth. So he'd mince them up for him, put a bit of onion and carrots and stuff. And just fry them. That's the only way Dad could eat them, couldn't chew them. And when we was out on the rocks we used to just cook them in the shells, have the ashes and clean them and smash them and put them in the shell with salt water and cook them like that.

Sue: Cook them for long?

Carol: No only a minute on each side cause if you cook them for too long they go rubbery. We used to cook them in butter.

Sue: Was BJ earning good money from it, was it worth a lot of money?

Carol: No it wasn't much. It was so much a bin. It wasn't really a lot; it's a lot now but not then.

Sue: Was it hard to cope on the income or was it comfortable?

Carol: It was OK because you lived on credit. We used to book up at the shop. It was sort of hard because you were living in a housing commission house and you'd get behind with your rent but you couldn't explain to them that you would pay it when they were working. But we managed to pay it, like you'd get a little bit behind, but you'd catch up. It was a bit hard especially in the rough weather because sometimes they wouldn't get out for a week you wouldn't get any income at all. Only around the rocks we'd get in the shelter and get a few here and there. Go all day and scrape up a bag to just keep going. And I think he went on sickness benefit for a while and then he went into the Land Council.

Sue: Do you miss them, the abs?

Carol: Yeah we still get a feed, Bobby [son in law] usually drops us in a feed of abs and a lobster. So we're still getting our seafood. BJ doesn't really have time to go now; he doesn't do much diving at all. The tide's got to be out and he can't go deep. At Christmas time he went out, he can't go real deep because he gets sick and his ears ache. The boys usually drop us some. When Ty [nephew] was here he was getting us mussels and fish, so we still get our seafood.

Sue: Continuing the tradition. You're the older ones now.

Carol: Young fellows make sure; I think he gets Mum and Dad their lobster every month and a few abs.

Sue: It's harder now isn't it?

Carol: Yeah with the fisheries, they're allowed to take their ten now, I think they going to try to drop that down to five. So if you've got a big family, for most of them that's been used to abalone. I think it was two lobsters that were allowed and I think they're dropping that down to one too. [6]

The changes in fishing licence arrangements have affected many Aboriginal people on the south coast. Ernie Brierly carried on the family tradition of commercial fishing going back to the early whaling days of his grandfather, Walter Oswald Brierly, at Twofold Bay. He had a trawler and would go to Eden and Ulladulla to work, using Moruya as a home base. His three sons continue the work. Considering their busy fishing lives we were lucky to find Ernie, his wife Beryl and son Alan in Moruya at Alan's house.

Ernie: Wouldn't catch the kids awake for three months on the ocean. Used to come home to see them and she wouldn't let me wake them up. And me Uncle would always try to catch me in bed, he'd come round, he'd waltz in the door at three o'clock and say, 'I got him in bed.' Beryl'd say, 'Who?' He'd say 'Ernie.' 'He must be nearly in Eden b' now.' A week after that he died. He could never catch me in bed, but now they can. Even if I feel sick in the daytime, in the night- time I still want to go fishing. Going out tonight with the boys get the net ready, get everything ready.

Beryl: Alan do you still fish too?

Alan: Yeah we got the licence, John, Wayne and I, we all got licence.

Liddy: Got your own boat?

Alan: We've got six boats registered and we use the lot of them, just cruise in and grab a boat, still keep the business. We've mainly been getting garfish at the moment. John's up in Illawarra now, he's up there trawling. Just getting a few mullet out of the rivers, mainly bream, just meshing.

Ernie: When we start we get all kinds of fish because we never done much since Christmas. The tourists and that come. We've got gear for everything, any kind of fishing you want to do; off the wharf, in the rivers, meshing.

Alan: When I first went fishing, I was 14 and nine months. I left school; fishing licence then was only worth $2. From $2 it jumped up to $100 and from $100 to $575. Now you got to put in for another one it's going to cost me, our family go fishing it's going to cost seven grand next year, for all year to go fishing. It's the endorsements now like they got a beach hauling endorsement, an estuary endorsement.

Ernie: Half these ones here you ask them they couldn't tie an half hitch knot around a post. Put them in a boat and they row backwards in it.

Alan: Everything we know, the old man taught us. Like all the fishermen know. That's why we keep the licences for to hand them down. We're not going to sell them; we're going to pass them down. The only way we're going to get out of the business is the three brothers get together and say, Righto we're going to sell up. And the way things are going we might have to do it because like $7,000 a year. We're scraping up 500 bucks a week to work in it already. And that's just to pay your rent and board. So in other words the government is pushing us out that way. The money way, it's more for the big companies. The individuals now they're trying to push us out in other words. When I left high school on my licence I was allowed to get abalone, lobsters, everything, straight out of the water except perch or school sharks, you weren't allowed to catch them, endangered species.[7]

Bag Limits

From the time of the restriction of the abalone fishery in NSW (1980) prices have continued to rise and it's now a big money industry. In 1967–68 the in-shell price for abalone was 14.5 cents per pound (about 30 cents a kilo). By 2000 the beach price was about $50 per kilo and the average catch rate for commercial divers was about 20 kilograms an hour, paying them $1000 an hour. The total commercial catch in NSW in 2000 was 305 tonnes (305,000 kilos) divided up between 42 shareholders in what is now a share-managed fishery. This is big business, especially when it's remembered that 99% of that tonnage is for export, leaving local buyers to rely on the black market which pays over $100 per kilo.[1]

NSW Fisheries now commit considerable time and effort to policing the regulations governing the abalone fishery. For south coast Koories this has meant that their traditional food gathering behaviour has become suspicious and they are harassed by Fisheries officers who check bag limits, sizes and whether the abalone have been shelled straight after being caught.

As Ossie Cruse explains:

> So in the process of making an industry of abalone the NSW government took away from Aboriginal people traditional rights of gathering our traditional foods. And also made it illegal for us to process our food the way we've processed it for thousands of years. As a result people are being fined for what they call shucking the abalone on the rocks which was the traditional way where you took it out of the shell and then tenderised it by taking a smooth rock and pounding the flesh and washing it

clean and bringing it home that way. And cooking it in the traditional way, it was a lot tenderer than letting the abalone die in the shell.[2]

Many south coast Kooris have had run-ins with the Department of Fisheries over these regulations and they are feeling the pressure. Paul Hudson and Newton Carriage come from the tradition of abalone gathering.

Paul: They're watching you all the time, if you're black that's it, they mark you. Like, I camped down Mystery Bay like after Christmas for holidays with the kids, I went down at half past five in the morning to get a feed of mutton fish and the Fisheries were sitting up in the cliff watching me at half past five in morning.

Sue: It must be hard around here because it is built up so much all around the coast where you would have been able to just go and get the abalone.

Newt: Oh yeah, as soon as you get into the water along the coastline now, especially with the houses, they have a thousand dollars reward to dob in a poacher and people are probably watching you, retired mob from Canberra, sitting there just

Shane and Newton Carriage, with Keith Nye (background), cleaning mutton fish at Bateman's Bay, 1989.

looking straight up, you know. Even before you get any abs they're right on top of you in their boats.

Paul: They got a plane now that flies up and down the coast, Fisheries, and they spot you, spotter plane and they just ring the Fisheries and that's it, they're there in . . . well, you got to remember that they're only about fifteen minutes apart, to get to you no matter which part of the ocean you're in, they're there.

Beryl: Yeah, and no one will knock back a thousand dollars either, that's a lot of money.[3]

Darren Mongta grew up in Eden and learnt to dive with BI and Dennis Cruse. He still gathers abalone and finds the bag limit of ten per diver a frustration.

Darren: Ah, it's very upsetting for me I get really upset with it all, with the whole lot of it. I wish they could give us some sort of decent rights to them. I mean ten's a feed but what about the elderly people like you [Beryl] and my mother. They can't dive, and they love the abalone. The other day when we went to the funeral at Wallaga; Uncle Doonie said to me, he was crying on me shoulder, he said, 'Uncle,' he said, 'I haven't had a feed for nearly about eight years. Can I have a feed of . . . , can you bring me a feed of muttonfish, even if it's one! Can you please bring me one abalone, I don't get none!' And I just felt that bad. Troy had a couple there he took up for Uncle Penno. I said, 'Give me two abs, please I'll take it over to give to Uncle Doonie.' Look he was just crying, just for that two abs. He was so happy.

Fair enough, some of them do go and get them to sell. For ones that are struggling and have got no food in the cupboard sometimes know that they can go down to the sea and get a feed.

Beryl: But you've had the fishing inspectors waiting on you, haven't you?

Darren: Oh, they're at the house. You see them come past the house all the time. I have a few friends come out one week;

we have a barbeque, or something. I say, we'll go and get a feed of abalone, go for a dive and get a feed and that. We'll come back, hang the wetsuits on the fence, we're having a barbeque. They'll come up, turn around. Ah, it's like they're harassing you. Sometimes I feel like just jumping out of my car and going off my head, but they're probably waiting for me. They're probably just saying, 'Well this is what we want him to do, you know, so we can get him into trouble.' You know, I don't do that anymore I just get a feed. I used to get a few now and then, but I just want a feed you know.

When [I was kid] I used to sit on the rocks watching, waiting for Dennis and them to get out of the water, sometimes you'd have the white people walking past and I'd be sitting there playing with them, you know. They'd be, 'Err, yuck, look at what these guys got.' Then they'd be saying to their kids, 'Get away yuck yuck they've got that yucky snail things there, don't, look they're going to eat 'em.' And I'm sitting there, 'what are these coots talking about, these are lovely.' They didn't want nothing to do with them. But nowadays, once they realise how good for you they are, the Chinese and that, they use them for medicines, so you can imagine how good for you they are.[4]

Even when working as a fully licensed diver, Dennis Cruse was often checked more by Fisheries when out diving.

Darren Mongta and daughter Brooke, Eden, 1991.

Ossie: They ring up and report them. They were doing that to Dennis when Dennis was diving. Fisheries used to come up, two or three times a week, pull his boat over, search his boat. People used to report him, tell lies, they'd say he's got undersized abalone, thing like that . . .

Beryl: Yeah because he was getting a lot too, bringing a lot of abalone in. They thought he was paying other divers for it too. He had a licence. They had a big meeting in the CWA rooms because they thought he was buying abalone from other Koori divers.

Ossie: But Dennis used to dive with me when he was a kid, and he knew this coast, he knew where the best abs were, because we used to dive all the time, even when we came down to live here at Kiah we were still divers then, we used to sell our abalone to Owen Allan. He was a good diver Dennis, and a good seaman too, he knew the sea. He knew which way the roll was going to come the next day, and he'd go to that sheltered area go

Dennis Cruse, Eden, c. 1980s.

straight there. But it was a cultural change for us because that was one of our main resources for getting food on the table. A lot of people depended on abalone when we could sell them like that to the dealers. As soon as they brought the restricted licence in and restricted the numbers you could get that put a lot of people out of work. A lot of people because all along this coast Kooris used to be the main divers. And then when they started to hear about it more everybody got into it, kids and all. Not only Koori kids but gubba kids and all. It'll soon be classified as an endangered species if we don't do something about it. We've really got to look at ways we can produce the spawn and grow them in protected areas. In fact they should close off areas of this coast and make it out of bounds for diving, and police it so that the stock can come back. The Gulf of Mexico they fished it out so bad, and the Californian coast of America they had to close the seasons, make them out of bounds for diving. Commercial enterprise started to make them endangered species.

Ty Cruse, Ossie's grandson, tried to keep within the bag limit by only gathering ten abalone a day and storing them up in his grandmother's fridge. He was caught and charged with hoarding the abalone and given a twelve-month bond and his diving gear and the abalone were confiscated. He was able to get the gear back because the judge found that the NSW Fisheries Department had not adequately publicised the ban on hoarding and they were instructed to make this regulation more widely known.

Some Kooris on the south coast do work as poachers supplying the lucrative black market. Joe Carriage had been caught a number of times and his wife Laurel was also under surveillance by Fisheries officers.

> **Laurel**: I'm just saying, we up to Sydney to visit our daughter, we'd just come back from the north coast, we pulled in there in Redfern to see her and while we were there the police were in the TNT building, with the binoculars on our car, and as we drove out they pulled us up. And they said, 'Oh, we heard this is a poacher's car.' They stripped-searched our car and everything.
>
> **Joe**: My car is marked, every car I owned is marked.

Laurel: Even mine now.

Beryl: But that's right down the coast, I mean they pick others out; they got 'em picked out. They know them.

Joe: The Fisheries know their pros. In the poachers, who the pros are, who gets out, who can make it and who can't make it. Today everyone who goes along this coastline, no one can teach their boys, no one can go out and show their boys the traditional ways of hunting and gathering today, because the white man's stole everything away from us. It's hard when you take your own kids out and say, 'Come on let's have a dive.' You can't dive good, cause you're watching them all the time, while they're swimming around with you you're watching them, so they don't get caught with the ab iron. Because it's not as easy as people think, you know, getting hold and learning to dive, it's dangerous, I reckon the water's the most dangerous thing of life.

Laurel: This last one you're looking at jail.

Joe: Yeah, I might be looking at jail with this last one, because I got caught with the main person. But we'll come that as it gets here. But I've been caught four times. Fisheries have kept three lots of abs on me and I've won one lot of abs back. How we won that is I just give my name and address and I never said no more words from there on, if they asked me questions I shrugged my shoulders, sort of nod my head or whatever. I would not give them the satisfaction of using anything in court against me on my own words. So I thought I'd sit back wait for my solicitor, because I thought it's about time we get cunning and play it the same way they play it.

Beryl: But you can't clean them on the rocks how you used to prepare them, take them back to the older people in the community, you can get fined for doing that.

Laurel: We did that once on Aboriginal day, eh, at Barling's [Beach] there. They had a news camera and everything there. Fisheries were just too scared to touch us because there were too many of them. Everyone was diving in the water and they were getting the abs and lobster, they made a big fire and everything going on there. We only did this a couple of years ago.

Joe: There's one thing I've forgot to say, the problem with the Fisheries is they think that we go and get rid of our abalone to buy drugs.

Laurel: And they really believe that. Well the last time they pulled us up they searched our car for drugs. Got me and the kids out of the car and made us stand in the street . . . terrible embarrassing.

Joe: Yes, it's wrong, you know, and they make a big fool out of you, while there's a lot of people around. Cause they're the law, they've got the same law as the police, where they can walk in and play the hero boy. I just will not allow them to play the hero boy with me.

Sue: Do they bring the police in too?

Joe: If you be smart or whatever.

Laurel: Last time they did they took you to the police station.

Joe: Yeah, they had bullet proof vests and all on. They must have thought we were gangsters. And now look at them today, there's not one blackfella on the south coast who's got a licence and look at the money they're pulling. I reckon that's wrong, they say, years ago it was two dollars a licence. But now, if I knew what I know today, I would have had me licence and I would still be diving. I would have sold it. I'd be sitting back as a millionaire. I would have been a rich millionaire blackfella.[5]

Court Cases

> ... The real process of dispossession of these (fishing) rights has only begun to occur in the last 20 years as stocks of marine resources have begun to suffer serious decline. In time, it is likely that historians will record the treatment of Aboriginal people on the south coast of New South Wales by Fisheries' officers and police in much the same terms as Professor Henry Reynolds has described the actions of their 19th century forebears.[1]

Ever since the arrival of the white population non-Indigenous laws have entered into the relationship between the Kooris, their livelihood and the land and sea. As the rule of force was sheathed, the rule of law took over. This initially enforced the taking of traditional land with the Crown claiming all land and leasing or selling it to squatters and settlers.

This was followed by the paternalistic management of Aboriginal people by the Aborigines Protection Board which controlled Koori lives with extensive regulations, curtailing their freedom of movement, association, employment and access to traditional culture.

After 1967 Aboriginal involvement in management organisations developed with the National Aboriginal Congress, the NSW Lands Trust and, more recently, the NSW Aboriginal Land Councils which were brought into being through the 1983 *Land Rights Act (NSW)*. These operate under the three tiers of local, regional and state-level councils. Unoccupied Crown land was available for land claims until 1998 and the organisation was funded through a percentage of land tax levied by the state government.

Increased involvement by Aboriginal people in their own business is undoubtedly an advance over the earlier methods of control but there is frustration with the system due to having to juggle the community's needs and rights within the overriding white legal system. There is a feeling of distrust and a desperate desire to achieve material and social gains quickly.

Using the collective power of the Land Council, the members of the Narooma Local Aboriginal Land Council undertook a series of court cases to establish their right of access to abalone, based on the traditional use of the resource. Ronnie Mason, then chair of the Narooma LALC told us how his brother Kevin Mason felt he was being constantly harassed by Fisheries and that this drove them to take matters into their own hands.

> **Ronnie**: Like I say, Kevin's the first black fella in Australia who's been to jail for it. The guy went to jail for trying to get a feed for his family. They've chased Kevin around, it's probably well known, surveillance on him and all this stuff, and they used to talk like the bloke's got a million quid, and he had the arse out of his strides, bit of an old bomb car you know.
>
> So we said look what we'll do, we'll go and get a licence. So, me and Normy Patten, Keithy and them blokes, we went and got a licence for ourselves. And the first day we dived out at Camel Rock with a licence, Fisheries come along and pinched us because we had two undersized lobsters and the normal procedure, what they do if they pull you up the first time, because it was the first time we were pulled up with it since we got a licence, is give you a warning and throw the little ones back you know. What he's done, he's taken it off us, charged us, took us to court. And this is where all these court cases started off.
>
> I said well stuff you fellas, I don't know what you blokes are going to do, I'm pleading not guilty to this business, I'm not putting up with this harassment, and that's where we started, our first court case was the lobster one and it went for four years, yeah. But, they beat us in court, at least we've made them sit up and have a look at us, we're not going to sit back and take all the bull off them, being harassed. We run the next case with my young bloke, Ronald. The second case, they knocked us over on

that one too. But they're going to appeal on it through the Mabo legislation see, come back with that.

See, what we did in the first place, we run it as just two individuals, me and Normie Patten run it so we had no legal standing, like a European sort, you know. They knocked us over on those technicalities. So we run the next one as the family one, that was the one I run with Ronald. So if they do knock us over on this one, then we're going to go on the traditional one then, you know with a nation of people.

Beryl: But you can claim a long association from your childhood and back . . .

Ronnie: Oh yeah. But they knocked us over on a couple of technicalities, but like I say if we're going to go Mabo, hit them with that one, well we got all the history there you know, that's all we got the association, with the family ties through right down. Well, that's what I said to these fellows, when we first starting talking, quite a lot of them, they said, 'Oh, no, I don't want to do it.' I said, 'Mate, you got to be prepared to go to jail over this you know. You got to put your hand up, one bloke puts his hand up, you all got to put your hands up, mate, if you want something.' Otherwise they walk all over you if you're just one person, one or two of us, yeah.[2]

The big change in the disputes over rights to abalone came with the Mabo High Court decision in 1992. Before Mabo, Australian law held that the land before 1788 was terra nullius, meaning it belonged to no one. This was based on the mistaken perception that Aboriginal people didn't own the land because they didn't till the soil to reap or harvest — a Eurocentric view of the hierarchy of people, which put Englishmen at the top of the heap.

The Mabo decision allowed for Native Title in land and adjacent seas that fulfilled certain requirements as laid down in the High Court ruling and the later *Native Title Act*. These required that:
1. Native interest can only be claimed if it can be shown that it existed immediately before 1788.
2. Native interest must be a recognisable part of a system of rules observed by an identifiable group connected with a particular locality.

3. Persons claiming interest must show biological descent from the group observing the system of rules pre 1788 or when the area was settled.
4. They must show that descendents of this group have and are still continuing to observe the system at the time the claim is asserted.
5. Such claims can only apply to certain kinds of unalienated crown land.

In 1991 Ronnie's son, Ronald Mason, was caught with 92 shucked abalone at Dalmeny. When the case, *NSW Fisheries v. Ronald Gordon Mason* was heard in the local court at Sutherland in May 1993 the defence was as follows:

1. That it has been the traditional custom since time immemorial to fish coastal waters for abalone and other fish to provide a major source for food.
2. This traditional custom has continued to be practiced and the Aboriginal people of the south coast now have a traditional right to fish coastal waters and take abalone and that such right is recognized by common law.
3. The defendant is Aboriginal and a descendent of those Aboriginal people.
4. Fisheries and Oyster Farms Act and regulations do not evince an intention to take away customary Aboriginal rights and so the relevant provisions of the Act have no application to the defendant so he cannot be charged.

This case was lost and taken to the Supreme Court in 1993 where it was expanded into a group action and included reports by anthropologist, Scott Cain, and archaeologist, Sarah Colley, into the genealogies of the defendants and records of abalone use both pre and post-settlement. This was dismissed with costs.

> **Joe**: There was one, two, three. I'd better tell you the names eh? There was Keith Nye, there was Nicky Carter, there was Andrew Stewart, Mark Chatfield, Kevin Mason, young Ronnie Mason. And we all went to try to reopen the thing on Mabo, for hunting and gathering rights. It went on for a fair while and we thought we'd have victory, because it was something everyone on the south coast was supporting. It was about time we got up and done something.

Laurel: The establishment was supporting you too, the land councils and all them.

Joe: With the people what were going through it we all thought we'd walk out freely without a fine, without anything. But all got nicked; the State Land Council ran out of money they couldn't back the money anymore. Which I think was very wrong, because we're their black people, we should be their number one priority, of the south coast. That is our food. That is our hunting section. On the sea land, they should support anything that give native title to the sea to the black people, to let them go and give themselves a feed. But, it never worked out the way we wanted it to work out. We all went to court. We all got heavily fined. I think out of my two cases I got about a thousand something dollars, I don't reckon I should pay anything.[3]

In 1994 the case went to appeal where it was again defeated. It was held that Ronald Mason failed to establish that he was exercising a traditional fishing right because he gave no evidence of:
a) Any recognisable system of rules for the taking of abalone, nor
b) How his activities fell within the scope of such rules.[4]

The Appeal also held that Ronald Mason '... established the ingredients necessary "in law" to succeed in a claim for Native Title in respect of a right to fish. But he failed to provide sufficient evidence to prove that he had been exercising such a native title.'[5]

The difficulty here would seem to be that evidence of a recognisable system of rules for the taking of abalone would have to come from the accounts of early contact experiences of explorers and settlers. As discussed earlier, the records of use of abalone/mutton fish are very scanty. This is not restricted to the gathering of seafood. Most food gathered by women and children was poorly noted in the ethnographic record.

In the ruling for the Supreme Court judgment it was pointed out that traditional use of abalone didn't include commercial activities. This seems like a Catch-22 situation where the south coast Kooris can be denied access to their traditional food because it is now totally commercialised. Despite the increased technology, abalone and lobster fishing is still a hunter/gatherer activity.

Ronnie: But it's been hard for us to fight it because of the Abalone Association, you know, multi-million dollar business. They just got too much money, got too much political clout with Governments and all that. But the last couple of months I think we've been starting to talk to the Abalone Association blokes, you know. They've started to come over to our side sort of, because they know we're not going to go away.[6]

In the Mabo1992 High Court ruling Justice Brennan stated that '. . . . when the tide of history has washed away any real acknowledgement of traditional law and any real observation of traditional customs the foundation of native title has disappeared . . .'[7]

However there are signs that the official response to the Kooris' use of abalone and lobster is changing and making some allowances for traditional practices. Paul Hudson describes his experience.

Paul: About sixteen months ago, my other brother comes from Cowra and he was with me one day at Narooma, down at Fullers there and we were getting a feed because family from Victoria were coming over too, actually it was for our wedding. We ended up with too many and Fisheries caught us and they worked it out that there were ten per person. My two little girls, I was teaching them how to get them off the rocks with a screwdriver and they were all getting them off rocks and the Fisheries were watching us do it and then they caught us afterwards. We had twenty-nine more than we should have and that resulted in court and that. Two weeks ago it went to court and we pleaded guilty, the solicitor said that there is no way possible that you can get out of it, so we pleaded guilty. I explained to the magistrate that I was teaching the children how to get them off the rocks and the solicitor spoke with him for a lengthy period, and we pleaded guilty to it and he turned it around and he said, 'Well you've gathered them in a traditional manner and they weren't for sale, they weren't for the market, black market', and he said, 'I find that you did practise in a traditional manner and it was only for food, not for sale and you weren't liable to offend again.' So he said, 'I find you not guilty' and all charges were dismissed, no conviction. And I'm still working out with Fisheries yet to get my mutton fish back see . . . so they've got to return it.[8]

Joe Carriage, abalone hunter, 2004.

The Narooma men are still fighting for their rights to take as many abalone and lobsters as they want and to shuck and clean them by the sea. A case being heard in May 2004 (and which is still in progress) argues that gathering abalone and rock lobsters is a cultural activity on the south coast and that Aboriginality 'amounts to a religion, so stopping their hunter-gathering is arguably an attack on their religious freedom.'[9] There are eleven defendants facing a total of twenty-one separate charges carrying fines of up to $10,000 each and/or three months jail. If they lose they will most likely appeal and take the argument up to a higher court.

The Future

We've got to think about conservation too, for the resources, natural resources. But the point is, the argument that they're putting up is that we didn't deplete the stock, we didn't cut all the trees down that was the habitat for the goanna, you know, made them die out. That was farmers and graziers, they did that. And the same thing they did now with mutton fish or abalone. We didn't put in that big industry where they can take tonnes and tonnes of abalone a year, to deplete the stock. And yet we've got to pay the penalty of not being allowed to gather more than ten.

I've been reading BJ's report from that conference . . . and see the world's started to signal the problems on the ozone. . . that we're in trouble in this world not only for the pollution of the environment but for the way that we're managing the environment. There's an incredible rate of animal and plant life extinction in Australia. Every month there's a new endangered species because of the way we are treating the environment. I went to the bio-diversity meeting in Canberra and I was the only blackfella there, and they were talking about all the plant life in Australia that hasn't been tapped and when I asked about who were the delegates, you know who most of the delegates were? They were pharmacists. All they were worried about was how they're going to get drugs, pharmaceuticals. So they're in there. They're drafting their laws now. The bush medicine will disappear soon it'll be gone. I had to tell them I've got to break the law to get bush medicine. I've got to go into places like, it's only growing in the parks and wildlife areas.[1] (Ossie Cruse)

The Future

In the process of conducting the interviews for this book we asked each person what their vision was for the future. The question centred on the access to abalone as a resource for the Aboriginal communities of the south coast of NSW. However, *Mutton Fish* has been just as much about the beach culture of the coastal people, and the future involves the continuation of that culture.

Each generation of Kooris on the coast have seen major changes in their lives as government policies and commercial pressures have taken their toll on the traditional ways of life. Today we are more aware of the impacts on the environment itself as resources become scarcer and long-term weather patterns change. There are major effects on the abalone resource with over-fishing, increasing numbers of sea urchins taking over abalone beds and infestation by the parasite, *Perkinsus*, believed to be exacerbated by sewerage outfall from the large cities which has lead to the closure of commercial abalone fisheries from north of Sydney to Jervis Bay.[2]

Many people we spoke to complained that their traditional food has been depleted through the actions of the commercial industry, which has just focused the resource into the hands of a restricted number of hunter-gatherers and assisted in marketing abalone and the policing of non-licenced divers. Not only have the Kooris not benefited through this industry but they are often the ones found in court facing charges of poaching abalone.

A popular vision of the future was a change in the law to recognise Aboriginal rights.

Beryl: What would you like to see Ronnie (Mason), for the future as far as abalone and that?

Ronnie: Oh, I'd like to see what they're trying to do give us; each Land Council, each community, a licence and they're responsible for that licence. They got to catch no small stuff, it's all got to be all to size. If someone's family's come down from Sydney and they want to go and dive for some, say there's a permit, you go down and get them. But you've got to be also responsible for it if you get the little stuff you know. That's the only way you're going to do it.

Beryl: So you'd still like to see it done legally through a permit.

Ossie Cruse coming up from a dive, Eden, 1995.

Ronnie: Well, I think so. That's the only way; otherwise like I was saying, twelve months down the track they'll clean them out. You got to educate those fellows or they just get out and don't care. But I think this, the Fisheries and the Abalone Association, because it's a multi-million dollars business for them too, that's their business too, and they'll want to come in and do that sort of stuff with us. I reckon that's the only way to go myself. And that way, if we all got licences, this community, we police it too then, we police our young people.

Liddy: Have our own lot of rangers, yeah?

Ronnie: Yeah, all that. Well, like I say, at least you can go down and get a feed then, for the old people and that. I was going down this Umbarra [cultural centre at Wallaga Lake] down here, I was going to start this bit of traditional tucker and seafood, for the people when they go up the mountain. They saw the Fisheries people and said, 'Can we go and get some mutton fish?' Nope! [They] said you'd have to go to the Minister.

Go above them and get it done. That would be the thing if too, you've got something cultural going down at Eden there, you are allowed to go and get the food out of the sea and lakes, that people eat.

Beryl: Could that come through Mabo because I don't really understand that much.

Ronnie: Well, what we're talking down here, this is only state right. Now a Mabo, if they get it through the Mabo it will go all over Australia, right.

In 1997 more than 120 claims for sea rights were made all around Australia. These included two on the south coast that were accepted by the Native Title Tribunal for mediation. A claim by the Crocker Island people was going to be heard in the High Court as a test case This led to an outcry from commercial fishing groups saying that exclusive rights threatened the $1.8 billion industry. Galarrwuy Yunupingu from the Northern Land Council said that Crocker Island claimants were seeking recognition of their rights including protection of sacred sites and proper management of the resources on which their culture and subsistence depended.[3]

By October 2001 the High Court handed down its decision when five out of the seven judges agreed that the Aboriginal people of Crocker Island had native title over the seabed and the sea. However six out of the seven rejected their exclusive rights over the area, thereby giving precedence to commercial interests. This means that the law at least recognises that Aboriginal people have an interest in the management and allocation of fishing rights and licences.[4] This recognition will have to be reflected in a practical way by state ministries throughout Australia.

BJ: And the problem I have with the Mabo title is that before Mabo, Aboriginal people had right to what they called proper and just settlement. And you have rights to those things because of your birthright. But native title took that away from that now and native title says that you will have some form of settlement if you prove that you first are an Aboriginal person and meet certain criteria. You see the non-Aboriginal people set the criteria, it doesn't recognise birthright, doesn't take into account birthright. And also when you come up with proof, the proof that the courts are looking at is scientific, some cultural and historic. Well if you look at the historic proof then Aboriginal people were lucky if they went to school in this century let alone have any Aboriginal historians and people that could write things down at the time that all these things was documented, so all that stuff is documented by non-Aboriginal people for a start. And documented by a people that looked on Aboriginal people as a lower form of human being, they had certain attitudes about Aboriginal people. So these were the people that were recording things and saying things about us and these are the sorts of documents that the courts will be looking at.

I had different ideas bout that native title business in relation to licences, because to me, if you want access to those things because of your culture then how come there's so much emphasis on getting abalone licences, I mean, what about the pippies and the bimbulas? Why aren't we fighting for those things too? They are cultural things. [Is it] because they aren't worth as much money? I'm a little bit concerned that a lot of the issues weren't raised a long time ago when these things weren't worth money. And it seems like the thing that's worth the most money; it seems to be the one that has the most cultural significance for people these days. But I reckon that Aboriginal people should have licences, there should be a number of licences now, but how they get that you see.

Sue: How do you see things for the future, what's happening for the future?

BJ: Well the bottom line is, is that, some people bought their licences, Native Title or whatever, to me it doesn't matter, those people they should have a choice as to whether they want to get out of the industry themselves. If they do want to get out of it and the licence goes to a Koori then someone's got to pay for it. That's the way I see it. And I think that that's probably the way they're going to achieve something because the bottom line is that no matter what anyone does or how they come up with management plans for the ocean, the ocean's only going to have so much life in it at any one time. It's just like a paddock of dirt; you can only grow so much grass on it. And the government knows that there's groups of people that want some of that and have a right to it. And they break them up into categories, they probably considered the food chain, but I don't believe that the Kooris have asked for it in a way that the government can give. And they take into account that commercial divers have a right to a percentage of that resource stock there and they also take into account that there's got to be replenishment, so you've got to leave growth there to replenish the oceans. And tourists and recreational people want to access it too, so they want a percentage. So what it's going to come down to calculations based on predictions and estimates. And if we estimate that the oceans holds so much stock, then we need to identify a percentage that we're prepared to accept. And we say we want a percentage of that ocean, of that abalone, we want a quota. And then whatever Aboriginal people do with that quota, that's their business. And it doesn't matter that people weren't there to do their fish returns and all that sort of business, because the bottom line to me is that the abalone were there and they were there in abundance and blackfellas could take as much as they want and no one worried about it until they become worth money. And then they took it off Aboriginal people and they give it to the Japanese.

I don't like the idea that they say; you can have ten abalone quota, because a lot of people can't go get those abs. And there's no system in place for the old people to have their young people go and get their food chain for them like they used to. And the Fisheries is not going to give it to them and the ab divers are not going to give it to them and I don't think the Japanese people are gonna donate any back.[5]

In 2002 New South Wales Fisheries Department released their draft Indigenous Fisheries Strategy which aimed to 'foster a greater understanding of Indigenous cultural fisheries issues' and to encourage the involvement of Aboriginal communities in 'the management of the State's fisheries resources.'[6]

The final strategy and implementation plan, released in December 2002, was based on four key platforms of: respect for, engagement with, social and economic development and employment of Aboriginal people in fisheries activities throughout NSW. However the main focus seems to be on traditional cultural fishing practices, setting up an advisory committee and employing Aboriginal Fisheries officers to 'promote community commitment to regulations.'[7] Aboriginal commercial fishermen have expressed dissatisfaction with the consultation process and feel that their concerns about the financial viability of their businesses still haven't been met.

Traditional cultural fishing practices were formalised in 2003 with Ty Cruse being the first Koori to get a special permit to 'take, transport and possess 75 abalone and 10 rock lobster for the purposes of an indigenous ceremonial event'[8] from Fisheries Victoria for his mother's wedding feast. The process of getting the permit was extremely long-winded and it was only with the assistance of his grandfather, Ossie Cruse, that Ty was able to break through all the red tape.

After diving for the mutton fish, Ty and his family were stopped at a roadblock manned by Fisheries' inspectors and two police officers who set about checking every licence and permit and tipping the abalone out onto the ground to inspect for size and number. The specification in the permit of 'marking of catch' refers to the cutting of each mutton fish in the shell to prevent Ty from selling the catch (which he had no intention of doing). This effectively negated the cultural value of the catch, making it tough and inedible. The whole process showed the bitterness of the dispute over access to this resource and how far from the intention of the cultural concession the actual experience is.

Certainly some of the ideas put forward by our interviewees have not eventuated. Ronnie Nye, from the Mogo Aboriginal Land Council and from a long-time fishing family himself had been working on designing that future when we spoke to him in 1996.

> **Ronnie:** We're actually in the process now of trying to negotiate, with the president of the ab diver's association, he's been in contact with me. And they're starting to put cards on the table on how to stop it all [the poaching]. John Smythe, I think there's about 12 of them in that association down there and John's the president of it and he's pretty reasonable, he's talking about

Permit for Ty to take 75 abalone.

three abalone licences now; them buying us three abalone licences.

Beryl: Will that go to the local council, Aboriginal councils?

Ronnie: Well I hope not, because there's enough conflict in the communities without another conflict. There's going to be a major conflict in the community if it's accepted anyway because three licences along this coast is not enough.

Beryl: Well how would you do it with three licences then?

Ronnie: It would be very hard, there'd have to be another package besides those licences. One suggestion I put to them

Mutton fish cut in the shell, Wingan Inlet, Victoria, 2003.

was one of the problems they've got with the abalone, the grounds themselves. They're being taken over by the sea eggs. Why can't they supply us with boats, diving gear, compressors and everything and get them beds cleaned out.
And pay a wage, or so much a bag to remove them.

Sue: Why are they taking over though?

Ronnie: A sea egg comes in and there's no way an abalone can get in under a sea egg. Once he walks along he'll get into a hole and he'll just stay there. That's just it. They just move in. There's literally millions and millions of them, tonnes of them along this coast, sea eggs. John informed me that they've done trials on the clear outs and they're very successful. The thing is you've got to keep the people busy. In our community out at Mogo alone we've probably got twelve, fourteen divers that do it at some time or another. You get fourteen divers on nine tonne of abalone, which is worth about $450,000. They're going to knock that quota over in probably two months, three months. Then they're going to go back to their old ways again. And it's not going to work.

Beryl: So you'd have to police it too.

The Future

Ronnie: Yeah, it'd have to be policed. And you'd have to find an alternative for them after the quota was reached, something that's going to keep the money coming in to them. See it's different with the ab diver; see the ab diver's probably earning $450,000 a year. That's only one person, if you've got ten people, that's only $45,000 a year. And between those ten people you've still got your fuel, running costs, your deckhand. They've got to be nominated divers, under the scheme put forward by the abalone diver's association to the government, a nominated diver cannot be a person whose got a record for offences.

Beryl: How's that going to work then? There's a lot of Kooris now that have been fined.

Ronnie: That's right, they're going to have to rewrite the Act. They'll have to rewrite their laws. These are the sort of hurdles you've got to try and get over. But they've also got to look at the long term, not something in the short term, that's what I say. You know you've got probably got blokes out there who are earning $15–20,000 a year just on the side. Now. And if they're going to knock over their quota in three months, their little share, portion of it, what are they going to do for the other nine months? You can get all the undertakings signed that you like, once you've been doing something for twenty years, it's very hard to come back out of it. You know, it's something you just can't stop over night. I don't know where it's all going to end up but I hope it comes to some reasonable solution to work out for the both sides. As I said to the new director of Fisheries down here, I said people are getting sick of it. Just all band together and go and wipe them out, because you are going to wipe them out anyway.

Liddy: What did he say to that?

Ronnie: Jaw dropped down to the table.

Beryl: Well the professional divers are doing that now aren't they?

> **Ronnie**: That's right the problem that they've got is that Fisheries have put a legal size limit on them, the mutton fish. Now that legal size limit is taking all the breeders. They're not taking a little bit of the small stuff, and the majority of the big stuff, they just taking all the big stuff. They don't come into maturity until they're about five or six years old. And that's a long time to wait for more spawn to come. But we were trying to start up an abalone farm up here and we even told the fisheries we'd re-seed the ocean. Put the juveniles back. They said, no. You're not allowed to put nothing back into the ocean. But yet they can put scallops in Jervis Bay, out of a research station.[9]

The NSW Indigenous Fishing Strategy discusses the prospect of developing an aquaculture industry with the Aboriginal communities. This has long been discussed on the south coast with the NSW Land Council funding fact-finding trips to both New Zealand and Tasmania. NSW Fisheries have developed an abalone hatchery at the Port Stephens Fisheries Research Station, which can supply spat to aquaculture developments along the coast. In April 2000, the Wagonga Lands Council in Narooma announced they had been investigating establishing a multi-million dollar aquaculture venture on land they had acquired for that purpose. Part of the funding for the feasibility study came from the Canadian Government after Ronnie Mason's son Ron attended a seminar at the Canadian Consulate in Sydney where he found that, 'The Canadian Government is really supportive of its indigenous population and aquaculture.'[10]

Since 2001, a number of Aboriginal men from the south coast have been attending aquaculture training courses at Port Stephens run through TAFE. This is part of the NSW Fisheries' aims of supporting Indigenous communities in establishing aquaculture ventures.

Of course the commercial side of abalone is a recent development and most south communities are more interested in retaining their traditional access to the sea and its resources.

> **Darren**: I reckon they should at least take into consideration that, like what we're saying with the old people and that, it should be like the Maoris have got it. If we don't do something now, we're going to get nothing. The Maoris have got a piece of land, headland. They're able to look after that. That's something we

should, as a community, should do. Get together and, if we want our stock, like our food we like, our natural food we've been brought up on, our fish, and our mussels and oysters and abalone and lobster, we should get a bit of land, like Haycock or something, and look after it.

We'd definitely want to look after it, because I tell you what, I'd rather go in the sea and get abalone or fish than go up to the supermarket and buy a can of baked beans, or something in the can. The only food I eat out of a can is baked beans, 'cause I've been brought up on it. I won't eat anything else that comes out of a can. And the same thing with my food, I've been brought up with that food so I've got to have it every week. If I don't have my fish or oysters or mussels or something every week I get sick, I believe.

Beryl: Well we did that for years and the kids, likes of you and Dennis and my Dennis too and BJ. It was something that was there all the time and it was there, go and get a feed and that.

Darren: That's right, every weekend we'd always get together, families used to get together. We'd always do that weekend thing and it was so good.

Beryl: Well the law not only changed the food chain it's sort of broken that family gathering up, that we used to do and go out doing, make a day of it. Or even for a full weekend, we'd camp on the beach.

Darren: Yes, sometimes there'd be something like fifty, sixty Kooris in one little spot. And it was just unreal. Used to love chasing them, fishing, it'd be just fishing and diving everything to do with the sea.

In the last few years Koori families have been taking the summer holidays together camping at the cultural camps set up on the beaches through negotiation between the Land Councils and the National Parks and Wildlife Service. These have helped to retain the connection with the past beach culture by the community sharing the traditional knowledge in a natural way with the new generation coming up. Liddy's granddaughter, Daneika Stewart, has written about her experiences at the beach staying in the culture camp.

> Every year after Christmas, since 1998, we gather our camping gear and head out to camp along with other local Koori families. It usually takes three to four loads to get all our stuff out there. While the parents are setting up the camp us kids head out to explore and see if anything has changed. When we go exploring we usually look for the kangaroos, we have given some of the kangaroos names, for example Jake. Jake is the biggest kangaroo out of the whole mob at Haycock and we always check to see if he is still alive. After we finish exploring we go back to camp and have tea, then we run off again and follow the kangaroos through the bush. We go as far as we can. Once we chased the kangaroos really far into the bush, then suddenly Jake jumped out from some bushes and started to chase us! We ran through the bush and then climbed a tree. When we were sure Jake was gone we climbed down the tree and ran back to camp before it got too dark. As soon as we get back we grab the torches and look in the trees for possums. There are a lot of possums around our camp and some make some really loud noises at night. One night when my sister, Teneille, and me were sharing a tent with our cousin Alec, we heard a noise that sounded like an old lady laughing; it was the freakiest thing I've ever heard. We went outside to investigate and when we couldn't find anything we got scared and literally jumped in our tent.
> When we got sick of looking for possums we sat around the fire, toasting marshmallows on a stick while my Dad and Uncle Steve played their guitars and tried to get us to sing. When they were tired of singing we all told yarns. Sometimes they were funny but most of the time they were scary. When we tell ghost stories everyone gets nervous and moves closer to the fire. As we tell ghost stories everyone goes to bed one-by-one until there is no one left. Sometimes at night everyone gets their torches and we go bush walking. There was this one time when my mum and dad took all us kids for a walk at night and my Uncle Steve and Uncle Don put these masks on and scared us.
> When morning comes it's usually the kids who wake up first and visit the other camps to see if the kids from the other

The Future

Brodie, Teneille and Daneika Stewart at the culture camp, Haycock, 1999.

families are up. When we go back to camp one of the adults is usually awake and has a fire going. We get dressed and have our brekky and wait for the other adults to wake up so we can go to our destination. On most days we go to a secluded beach that only our family knows about and fish, swim and go snorkelling. Sometimes we go to other beaches such as Severs or Barmouth. Sometimes we go to this place up from our camp to fish. To get there you have to climb down a little cliff as it is on the rocks. Once when me and my cousin Alec were on our way back to the camp we were scared by a brown snake. We were climbing the cliff, talking, when Alec yelled out, spun around and pushed me down the cliff. I started screaming and when I heard Alec yell, 'snake' I screamed even louder. When we reached the bottom we heard my dad yelling his head off. It was pretty funny.

Out at camp we eat a lot of fish and mutton fish, because when we go to the beach someone always fishes and dives for dinner. We love the days when Nan stays back at camp because at the end of the day when we are really starving Nan always has a big feed of warm fried scones and lovely ash dampers already for us, which we usually have with golden syrup. They are beautiful. When we have mutton fish my Dad prepares them by smashing them in a tea towel and frying them on a hot plate. Once my Uncle Ak caught a spotted cod which we call a boot and made a big curry-soup. Then we feed the leftovers to the goanna but not often because they have to eat their natural foods. A lot of goannas hang around our camp during the day. We always have to shut the food tent up or they will get in there first chance they get. One day Uncle Ak took the boys for walk into the bush and when they came back they had special wood to make boomerangs and spears with. Uncle BJ came down from the other camp and showed the boys how to straighten the spears at the fire.

We stay out camping for three to four weeks and we always have a good time but we are glad when we get home because of the hot showers and soft beds. As soon as we get home we like to watch TV and rest until the next time we go out to the camp again.

Beryl and her great grandson Mattari Walkun (Mutton Fish Man) April 2004, Eden.

Glossary

abalone (also mutton fish)	*Haliotis sp*
bimbulas	Sydney cockles
bombies	a reef or underwater rise in open water
bundis	hunting sticks
coolaman	wooden carrying bowl
damper	bread cooked in ashes
deckies	deck hands on fishing boats
hookah gear	compressor, hose and mask supplying air to the diver
Kooris	south-eastern Aboriginal people
Larpa	La Perouse, an Aboriginal settlement on Botany Bay
Littoral	coastal region
meshing	catching fish with a fine net
mia mia	simple shelter made of branches covered with bark or blankets.
midden	ancient food heaps investigated in archaeological sites
porcupine	echidna
SAFCOL	South Australian Fishing Co-operative Limited
sea eggs	sea urchins
shuck	to shell a shellfish

Mutton Fish

Thoorga (*also* Dhurga)	language group around Wallaga Lake near Bermagui
wondarmas	apple berries fruit of a scrambling vine
wobbegongs	sharks

References

Colley, S. 'The colonial impact? Contact archaeology and indigenous sites in southern New South Wales' in Torrence, R and Clarke, A (eds.) *Archaeology of Difference: negotiating cross-cultural engagement in Oceania*, Routledge, London, 2000, pp. 278–99.

Goodall, H. *Invasion to Embassy Land in Aboriginal Politics in NSW 1770–1972*, Allen & Unwin, Sydney, 1996.

Mulvaney, J and Kamminga, J. *Prehistory of Australia*, Allen and Unwin, Sydney, 1993.

Organ, M. *Illawarra and South Coast Aborigines 1770–1850*, Aboriginal Education Unit, University of Wollongong, 1990.

Notes

Preface

1 M Jones, *Tracks*, Renmark, South Australia [no date] p. 45

What the Middens Tell Us

1 RJ Lampert & PJ Hughes, 'Sea Level Change and Aboriginal Coastal Adaptations in Southern NSW', in *Archaeology and Physical Anthropology in Oceania*, vol. ix, no. 3, October 1974, pp. 226–235.

2 ibid.

3 S Bowdler, 'Bass Point: the excavation of a south-east Australian shell midden showing cultural and economic change', BA (Hons) unpublished thesis, University of Sydney, 1970.

4 ME Sullivan, 'The recent prehistoric exploitation of edible mussel in Aboriginal shell middens in Southern NSW', *Archaeology Oceania*, vol. 22, 1987, pp. 97–106.

5 R Jones, 'Why did the Tasmanians stop eating fish?', in RA Gould (ed.) *Exploration in Ethnoarchaeology*, p. 20; NJB Plomley (ed.), *Weep in Silence*, Blubberhead Press, Hobart, 1987, p. 224'; G Dumett, 'Diving for Dinner, some implications from the Holocene middens for the role of coasts in the late Pleistocene of Tasmania', in MA Smith, M Spriggs & B Frankhauser (eds), *Sahul in Review*, no. 24, 1993.

6 S Bowdler, 'Hunter Hill, Hunter Island', Australian National University, Canberra, PhD (unpublished thesis), 1979.

7 S Bowdler 'Hook, line and dilly bag: an interpretation of an Australian Shell midden', *Mankind*, vol. 10, pp. 248–58

8 GT Emmons, *The Tlingit Indians*, University of Washington Press, Seattle, 1991, pp. 174, 243, 251.

9 CE Dortch et al., 'Aboriginal Mollusc Exploitation in SW Australia', *Archaeology in Oceania*, vol. 19, no. 3, October 1984, p. 95.

10 Interview with Ossie Cruse, 11 November 1992, Eden, by Beryl Cruse.

11 S Colley, 'A pre- and post-contact Aboriginal shell midden at Disaster Bay, New South Wales south coast', *Australian Archaeology* 1997, 45:1–19.

¹² Interview with Sarah Colley, 24 June 1996, Eden, by Liddy Stewart and Sue Norman.

Early Contact

¹ Historical Records of New South Wales, vol. 1, *Wreck of the Sydney Cove*, p. 763, (2 April [near Merimbula] 'Kindly treated us with some shellfish') p. 765, (11 April 11 [Wallaga Lake] '. . . both the young and old were anxious to give us part of their shellfish').

² J Hunter, *An Historical Journal of Events at Sydney and at Sea, 1787–92*, 1793, p. 44 in R Lawrence, *Aboriginal Habitat and Economy*, Canberra, 1967, pp. 43, 196.

³ P Parker King, *Narrative of a Survey of the Intertropical and West Coasts of Australia performed between 1818 and 1822*, vols I & II, Murray, London, 1826, quoted in V Attenbrow, *Aboriginal Subsistence Economy on the Far South Coast of NSW*, BA Hons (unpublished thesis), Department of Anthropology, University of Sydney, 1976.

⁴ Referred to in M Organ, *A Documentary History of the Illawarra and South Coast Aborigines 1770–1850*, Aboriginal Education Unit, Wollongong University, 1990, pp. 148–51. A list of the words and their translations are:

Bourda	Shell	*Tchall*	Bubble shell
Koungourou	Helmet shell	*Koungouroun*	Cone shell
Tarowann	Toothed Shell	*Biaouli (Haliotis)*	shell
Leroko, madaii	Oyster	*Kanal*	Mussel
Tianbigara	Shell	*Pagnand*	Sea urchin
Maroumbra	Limpet	*Korougo*	Comb shell
Marangale	Rockhorn shell	*Madjawa*	Shell
Tola Toaura	Trochus shell	*Wooura*	Venus shell
Wanana	Mollusc	*Tehal*	Helix shell

⁵ S Wesson, *Aboriginal Whaling History Project*, National Parks & Wildlife Service May 1999.

⁶ RH Mathews 'Ethnological notes on the Aboriginal Tribes of New South Wales and Victoria', *Journal of the Royal Society of New South Wales*, 1904, vol. 38, pp. 252–3.

⁷ *Twofold Bay Magnet*, 28 June 1909.

⁸ M McKenna, *Looking for Blackfellow's Point*, UNSW Press. Sydney, 2002, p. 120.

⁹ O Brierly, *Journals, 1842–1844*, Mitchell Library, Sydney.

¹⁰ T Mead, *Killers of Eden*, Arkon, Sydney, 1973.

¹¹ Interview with Ernie and Beryl Brierly, and Alan Brierly, February 1998, Moruya, by Beryl Cruse, Liddy Stewart and Sue Norman.

Land

¹ G Bass, *Journal*, 1798 in Collins, D. *An Account of the English Colony in New South Wales*, Vol. 1, 1802, T. Cadell and W. Davies, London, p. 41.

² S Norman, personal observation, October 2002, in time of extensive drought.

³ M McKenna, *Looking for Blackfellow's Point*, p. 45, UNSW Press, Sydney, 2002.
⁴ M Organ (compiler), *Illawarra and South Coast Aborigines 1770–1850*, Aboriginal Education Unit, University of Wollongong, 1990. Relevant documents relating to this case are quoted in full in this compilation of sources.
⁵ H Goodall, *Invasion to Embassy Land in Aboriginal Politics in NSW, 1770–1972*, Allen & Unwin, Sydney, 1996; chapters 6–9 deal with this period in NSW land politics.
⁶ G Thornton, 'Aborigines–Report of the Protector, to 31 December 1882' *NSW Legislative Council Journal*, (Session 1883) Sydney, 1884, vol. 34.
⁷ 'Aborigines-Report of the Protector', pp. 79–80 and *Register of Aboriginal Reserves*, NSW State Archives, location 2/8349, pp. 77–80.
⁸ *Register of Aboriginal Reserves*, pp. 20–1.
⁹ Records of Sister Smith, unpublished, Bega Family Museum, Bega.
¹⁰ *Invasion to Embassy Land*, Goodall, pp. 147–8. Other protesters included Mrs H Stewart, Mrs Les Stewart and Mrs Agnes Davis.
¹¹ Interview with Ossie Cruse, Eden, 1992, by Beryl Cruse.
¹² Interview with Beryl and Ossie Cruse, Wonboyn, 1996, by Sue Norman and Liddy Stewart.

Livelihood

¹ Interview with BJ Cruse, Eden, 1997, by Sue Norman and Liddy Stewart.
² Recording by J Mathews, AIATSIS sound archives.
³ Andrew Sayers, *Aboriginal Artists of the Nineteenth Century*, Oxford University Press, Melbourne, 1994.
⁴ P Macgregor, pers. comm. 1998 (at the Museum of Chinese Australian History, Melbourne).
⁵ Shirley Fitzgerald, pers. comm. Sydney, 1997.
⁶ Shirley Fitzgerald, *Red Tape Gold Scissors*, State Library of NSW Press, Sydney, 1996, p. 60.
⁷ Interview with Ben and Sarah Cruse, take from a video interview made by Craig Cruse at La Perouse in the 1980s.
⁸ Interview with Ossie Cruse, November 1993, Eden, by Beryl Cruse.
⁹ Interview with Paul Hudson and Newton Carriage, Bateman's Bay, 1996, by Beryl Cruse, Liddy Stewart and Sue Norman.

Life on the Beaches

¹ Copies of these tapes have been deposited in the archives at the Australian Institute of Aboriginal and Torres Strait Islander Studies (AIATSIS) where they are available for further study.
² Dorrie Stewart, Bateman's Bay, 1997
³ Jean Squires, Camden, 1997
⁴ Interview with David Squires, Eden, 1997, by Beryl Cruse, Liddy Stewart and Sue Norman.

[5] Interview with Ronnie Nye, Bateman's Bay, 1996, by Beryl Cruse, Liddy Stewart and Sue Norman.
[6] Interview with Tina Mongta, Kiah, 1998, by Beryl Cruse, Liddy Stewart and Sue Norman.
[7] *The Divers* by Stanley Nean (unpublished).
[8] Interview with Ossie and Beryl Cruse, Wonboyn Lake, November 1996, by Liddy Stewart and Sue Norman.

Put in for a licence
[1] Interview with Ossie Cruse, Eden, 1993, by Beryl Cruse.
[2] Interview with David Squires, Eden, 1997, by Beryl Cruse, Liddy Stewart and Sue Norman.
[3] *Abalone Share Management Plan*, NSW Fisheries, February 2000.
[4] *Abalone Share Management Plan*, ibid p. 7.
[5] Interview with BJ Cruse, Eden, 1996, by Liddy Stewart and Sue Norman.
[6] Interview with Carol Cruse, Eden, 2000, by Sue Norman.
[7] Interview with Ernie, Alan and Beryl Brierly, Moruya, 1998, by Beryl Cruse, Liddy Stewart and Sue Norman.

Bag Limits
[1] *Abalone Share Management Fishery Annual Report, 2000/2001*, NSW Fisheries.
[2] Interview with Ossie Cruse, Eden, 1993, by Beryl Cruse.
[3] Interview with Newton Carriage and Paul Hudson, Bateman's Bay, 1996, by Beryl Cruse, Liddy Stewart and Sue Norman.
[4] Interview with Darren Mongta, Eden, 1996, by Beryl Cruse and Sue Norman.
[5] Interview with Joe and Laurel Carriage, Bateman's Bay, 1996, by Beryl Cruse, Liddy Stewart and Sue Norman.

Court Cases
[1] A Chalk, 'Aboriginal Fishing Rights on the South Coast of New South Wales', paper presented at the Turning the Tide Conference, Northern Territory University, 15 July 1993.
[2] Ronnie Mason interviewed, Narooma, 1996, by Beryl Cruse, Lissy Stewart and Sue Norman.
[3] Joe Carriage interviewed, Bateman's Bay, 1996, by Beryl Cruse, Liddy Stewart and Sue Norman.
[4] CJ Gleeson, JS Priestly and P Kirby, *Mason v Titton and another*, Court of Appeal 34 NSWLR 572 F.
[5] P Kirby. *Mason v Titton and another*, p. 594 G.
[6] Ronnie Mason interviewed. Narooma, 1996, by Beryl Cruse, Liddy Stewart and Sue Norman.
[7] J Brennan, *Mabo v. State of Queensland [no 2]* (60).
[8] Paul Hudson and Newton Carriage, interviewed Bateman's Bay Land Council, 1996, by Beryl Cruse, Liddy Stewart and Sue Norman.

[9] J Woodford, 'Hunters take a stand against fishing law', *Sydney Morning Herald* Tuesday 27 April, 2004, p. 2.

The Future

[1] Interview with Ossie Cruse and Beryl Cruse, Wonboyn, November, 1996, by Liddy Stewart and Sue Norman.
[2] Bob Lewis, abalone diver, Eden, pers. comm., 2002.
[3] D Jopson, 'Alarm over new native title push for sea rights', *Sydney Morning Herald*, 29 December, 1997, pp. 1 & 4.
[4] C Banham and D Marr, 'High Court in landmark rulings on Aboriginal sea rights', *Sydney Morning Herald*, 12 October, 2001, p. 5.
[5] Interview with BJ Cruse, Eden, 1996, by Liddy Stewart and Sue Norman.
[6] Draft NSW Indigenous Fisheries Strategy, p. 1, viewed at 24 July 2002, <www.fisheries.nsw.gov.au>.
[7] *Indigenous Fisheries Strategy and Implementation Plan December 2002*, p. 3, viewed at 15 January 2003, <www.fisheries.nsw.gov.au>.
[8] *Permit Fisheries Act*, Victoria Department of Primary Industry, 2 December 2003.
[9] Interview with Ronnie Nye, Mogo, 1996, by Beryl Cruse, Liddy Stewart and Sue Norman.
[10] Laurelle Pacey, 'Land council plans $10m fish farm', *The Canberra Times*, 3 April 2000, p. 5.

Index

Page references printed in *italics* indicate illustrations not discussed elsewhere on the page. Illustrations which are discussed elsewhere on the page, or in the surrounding span of pages, are not highlighted.

Abalone Association, 62, 63, 67, 88, 92, 96
Aboriginal Protection Board, 23–4
Aboriginal reserves, 23–5, 28
agriculture, *see* farming
Ah Chin, 30
Ah Chouney, 29
Ah Yeck, Dr, 29
air compressors, 59, 61
Allen, Owen, 59, 61, 62, 79
Andy, Basil, 50, 58
aquaculture, 100
Araganu, 26
archaeology and archaeological sites, 7–12, 21–2, 49–50, 52, 86
artworks, 16, *18*, 28, 30, *31*
Australian Institute of Aboriginal and Torres Strait Islander Studies, 27

bag limits, 72, 75–82, 95, 98–9
Barling's Beach, 25, 31, 81–2
barter, 41, 42–3, 51
Bass, George, 21
Bass Point, 8, 25
Bass Strait, 15, 17
Batehaven, 35
Bateman's Bay, 24, 25, 28, 33
Bawley Point, 25

beach culture, 31–53, 91, 101–4; *see also* campsites
beach-netting, 49
bean picking, 31–2, 53, 69
Beaver, Gordon, 59, 62
Bega River, 24
Bermagui, 45, 59, 62
bimbulas, 42
Black Ada's Swamp, 24
black market, 75, 80–2
Blackfellow's Lagoon, 24
boats, 40, 41, 61, 69, 72, 73; owned by entrepreneur Ah Chouney, 29; in traditional society, 7, 8
Bodalla region, 23
Bogong moths, 17
Boyd, Ben, 19
Boydtown, 19
bream, 42–3, 50, 73
Brierly, Alan, *19*, 72–4
Brierly, Beryl, 72–3
Brierly, Ernie, *19*, 20, 72–4
Brierly, Oswald, 19, 20
Brierly, Walter (Pardi), 20, 38, 59
Brierly, Walter Oswald, 20
Brierly family, 20, 35–8
Brou Lake, 26
Broulee, 36
Broulee Beach, 50

113

Broulee Island, 38–40
Brush Island, 21
Bunga, 66
Burrill Lake, 8
bush medicine, 90
bush tucker, 26, 43–4; *see also* gathering methods; preparation methods; traditional custom

Cain, Scott, 86
Camel Rock, 45, 84
Campbell, Buddy, 26
camps, cultural, 25, 101–4
campsites, 24–6, 28, 31–53, 60; middens, 7–12, 21–2, 49–50, 52; *see also* Mystery Bay
Candlegut Beach, 36
canoes, 7, 8
Carriage, Joe, 80–2, 86–7, *89*
Carriage, Laurel, 80–2, 87
Carriage, Newton, 76–7
Carriage, Shane, *76*
catch sizes, 41, 50, 58, 62, 66; limits on, 63–4, 72, 75–82, 95, 98–9
Chapman, Henry, 41
Chapman family, 33–5
children, 33–53, 70, 88, 102–4; in traditional society, 4, 5, 6, 9
Chinese people, 29–31, 52
coastline, 7–8; map, *xiii*
Colley, Sarah, 10–12, 86
commercial operations, 35–8, 40, 49, 50, 52–3, 57–75, 78–80, 96–100; Abalone Association, 62, 63, 67, 88, 92, 96; Chinese, 29, 30–1, 52; environmental effects, 90, 91; poaching and poachers, 67, 76–7, 80–2; sea rights claims and, 93; whaling, 17–20, 35; *see also* divers and diving; trade
compressors, 59, 61
conflict with white settlers, 22–3
conservation, 74, 80, 90–1, 94–5, 98, 100; *see also* licences and permits
court cases, 23, 80, 84–9, 93–4
crayfish, *see* lobsters
Crocker Island people, 93
Cruse, BJ, 58–9, 62–3, 64–72, 77, 93–4, 104

Cruse, Ben, 30
Cruse, Beryl, 61, 79, 101; beach life, 34–8, 40–2; camping and campsites, 25–6, 49–53; photographs, *35*, *104*
Cruse, Carol, 69–72
Cruse, Dennis, 58, 59, 62, 66–8, 69, 70, 77, 78–80; as boy, 51
Cruse, Ossie, 57, 79–80, 96; campsites lived and worked in, 25–6, 49–53; compressor, 61; on conservation, 80, 90; photographs, *51*, *92*; trade with Chinese people, 30–1, 52; on traditional use, 10, 26, 75–6
Cruse, Sarah, 30
Cruse, Serina, 70
Cruse, Ty, 72, 80, 96
cultural camps, 25, 101–4
Currarong, 25
Cuttagee, 25

damper, 33–4, 103
Davidson family, 18
Davis, Percy, 27
de Sainson, Louis Auguste, 16
Department of Fisheries, *see* Fisheries Department
Depression, 33–5
digging sticks, 4, 15
Disaster Bay, 11–12, 42, 49–53
disease, *see* health and disease
diving and divers, 41–2, 46–9, 57, 58–72, 77–82, *89*, *92*, 98–100; for Chinese entrepreneurs, 30; Fisheries Department inspections, 78–80, 84, 96; for lobsters, 41, 84; in traditional society, 9, 15; women, 9, 37–8
diving equipment, 60–1, *63*; air compressors, 59, 61; goggles, 58; suits, 37, 61, 65–6
draft Indigenous Fisheries Strategy, 95–6
drawings and other artworks, 16, *18*, 28, 30, *31*
Duren, Jane, 24
Durras, 25, 62

East Gippsland, 15
Eden, 49, 50, 59, 60, 62, 72, 77;

Index

traditional society, 16; whaling museum, 18
employment and livelihood, 17–20, 27–32, 33, 57–74; *see also* diving and divers; seasonal work; wages and pay
equipment, 34, 70; agricultural, 53; Ossie Stewart's gathering tool, 45–6; in traditional society, 4, 7–8, 9, 21; *see also* boats; diving equipment
Esperance district, 9
European contact, xi–xii, 12, 15–32, 35

farmers and farming, 17–18, 19, 21, 22; conflict with, 23; market gardening, 29–30; *see also* seasonal work
First Fleet, 15
fish hooks, 7–8, 9
fish spears and spearing, 21, 42, 50
Fisheries and Oysters Act (NSW), 86
Fisheries Department, 75–82, 83, 92, 96, 99–100; court cases, 84–9; Indigenous Fisheries Strategy, 95–6, 100; *NSW Fisheries v. Ronald Gordon Mason*, 86–8
Fisheries Victoria, 96
fishing, 24, 27–8, 39, 59–60; for bream, 42–3, 50; in traditional society, 4, 7, 8–9; *see also* commercial operations; gathering methods; licences and permits
fishing lines, 4
fishing rights, 83–9
forest industry, 28, 33
free selection Acts, 23
French *Astrolabe* expedition, 16
fried scones, 37, 103
future, visions of, 90–104

garfish, 73
Garland Town, 36
gathering methods, 10, 88; recollections of, 32, 34, 41, 43, 50, 52; in traditional society, 4–5, 8, 15: whales, 17; *see also* diving and divers; equipment; fishing; preparation methods

geebungs, 44
Gerringong, 25
Gerroa, 25
gold mining, 23, 29
government policy, 23–4, 83; *see also* licences and permits
Green Patch, 25
Greencape, 42
Greenglades, 50

Hanging Rock, 25
Haycock, 102
health and disease, 17; abalone, 91; bush medicine, 90; divers, 67–9; herbalist doctors, 29
High Court decisions, 85–6, 88, 93–4
Hill Sixty, Port Kembla, 25
Holmes, Billy, 50
Holmes family, 42, 49
hooks, 7–8, 9
Hoskins, Jack, 24
Hudson, Paul, 31–2, 76–7, 88
Hunter, John, 15
hunting methods, *see* gathering methods

income, *see* wages and pay
Indigenous Fisheries Strategy, 95–6, 100

Jervis Bay, 16

Kalaru, 24
kangaroos, 5–6, 102
Kiah, 18, 20, 50, 79
Kiah River, 42
Kiama, 25
killer whales, 17, 18
Killers of Eden, 20
King, Phillip Parker, 16
King George V, 24
Kioloa, 25, 30

land, 21–6, 83; Native Title, 85–8, 93–4
land claims, 23–4, 83
Land Rights Act 1983 (NSW), 83
language, xi–xii, 16
laws, 23, 26, 75–89, 91–5, 99, 100

legal size limits, 100
licences and permits, 59, 63–4, 72–4, 82, 91–8; Fisheries Department inspections, 78–80, 84, 96
Little, Jimmy senior, 27
livelihood, *see* employment and livelihood
lobsters, 36, 37, 62, 69–72, 74, 82; court case, 84, 89; gathering methods, 41, 50, 60; traditional cultural fishing practices permits, 96, *97*; in traditional society, 8–9
Long Carry, 59
Lucas, Gordon, 59, 62

Mabo High Court decision, 85–6, 88, 93–4
Maoris, 9, 100
map, *xiii*
market gardening, 29–30
Mason, Kevin, 84–5, 86
Mason, Ronald, 84, 86–7, 100
Mason, Ronnie, 84–5, 88, 91–3
massacres, 22–3
Mathews, Janet, 27
Mathews, RH, 17
men, in traditional society, 3–4, 9, 15
Merimbula, 60, 61
Merriman, 23, 24
Mickey of Ulladulla, 28, 30
middens, 7–12, 21–2, 49–50, 52
mill workers, 28, 33
mining, 23, 29
Minora, 61
missions, 24, 25, 59; Wallaga Lake, 24, 27, 44, 92
Mogo, 30, 98
Mogo Aboriginal Land Council, 96
Mollymook, 25
Mongta, Darren, 77–8, 100–1
Mongta, Tina, 42–4
Mongta, Wally, 42–4
Moruya, 24, 35–6, 40, 41, 59, 61, 72
Moruya Heads, 39
moths, 17
murders, 22–3
Murramarang Point, 21–3
mussels, 8, 15, 42, 43, 72
mutton birds, 21

Mystery Bay, 25, *26*, 76; diving at, 58, 59, 65

Narooma, 88–9, 100
Narooma Local Aboriginal Land Council, 84
National Aboriginal Congress, 83
National Parks and Wildlife Service, 101
Native Title, 85–8, 93–4
Nean, Stanley, 46–9
Nerrigundah, 31
New South Wales Aboriginal Land Councils, 83, 101
New South Wales Fisheries Department, *see* Fisheries Department
New South Wales Lands Trust, 83
New South Wales State Land Council, 26, 87, 100
New South Wales Supreme Court case, 86–8
New Zealand, 9, 100
NSW Fisheries v. Ronald Gordon Mason, 86–8
Nullica people, xi
nutritional value, 8
Nye, Andy, 41
Nye, Keith, 76, 86
Nye, Ronnie, 41–2, 96–100
Nye family, 31, 41–2

orca (killer whales), 17, 18
oysters, 8, 27, 42, 43

Pambula, *29*
Parsons, Georgie, 39
pastoral industry, 17–18, 19, 21, 22, 23
Patten, Normie, 84, 85
pay, *see* wages and pay
pea picking, 45, 53
Pebbly Beach, 25
Pender, Jimmy, 58
penny winkles, 43
Penrith, Merv, 58
Perkinsus, 91
permits, *see* licences and permits
poaching and poachers, 67, 76–7, 80–2, 96
porcupine, 34, 44

Potato Point, 25, 32
Pre-contact, 3–12, 27
preparation/processing methods, 36, 38, 51, 70, 71, 103
  damper, 33–4
  traditional society, 4, *11*
  see also shucking
prices, xii, 58, 62–3, 69, 75, 98–9
  fishing licences, cost of, 73–4, 82
  see also wages and pay
Protector of Aborigines, 23–4

rabbits, 34, 39, 44
rations, 33, 34
recipes, *see* preparation methods
reserves, 23–5, 28
Robinson, George Augustus, journal of, xi
rock lobsters, *see* lobsters
Roseby Park, 24

SAFCOL, 59, 62, 63
salmon, 49
sawmills, 28, 33
scones, 37, 103
sea levels, 7, 8
sea rights claims, 93
sea urchins (sea eggs), 64, 91, 98
sealers, 17
seasonal work, 31–2, 45, 49, 50, 52, 69, 70; end of, 53; whaling, 18
seasonal resources, 17
sexual division of labour, 3–6, 8, 9, 15
shell middens, 7–12, 21–2, 49–50, 52
shootings, 23
shucking, 32, 62, 81–2
  court case, 86–8, 89
  Ossie Cruse's description of, 10, 30–1, 52, 75–6
size limits (undersize), 84, 100
  see also catch sizes
Smythe, John, 96–7
snorkel diving, 68–9, 70
Snug Cove, 16
songs, 27–8
spearing cattle, 23
spearing fish, 42, 50
spears, 21
species, xi–xii, 9, 15, 16

Squires, David, 38–40, 59–62, 64
Squires, Ernie, 59, 61, 64
Squires, Jean, 35–8, 59–60, 61–2
State Land Council, 26, 87, 100
Stewart, Daneika, 102–4
Stewart, Dorrie, 33–5
Stewart, Liddy, 25, *35*, 45–6, 102
Stewart, Ossie, 45–9
Stewart family, 26
storytelling and yarns, 6, 102
Supreme Court case, 86–8
swans, 43–4
Sydney cockles, 42
Sydney Cove, 15

1080 [poison], 59
Tasmania, 8–9, 100
technology, *see* equipment
timber industry, 28, 33
Tlingit Indians, 9
Tomakin, 24
trade, 10, 17; barter, 41, 42–3, 51; with Chinese people, 30–1, 52
traditional campsites, 25–6;
  middens, 7–12, 21–2, 49–50, 52
traditional cultural fishing practices permits, 96, *97*
traditional custom, 75–8, 84–104;
  (Ossie) Cruse on, 10, 26, 75–6;
  passing on of knowledge of, 10, 27, 42, 44, 46–9, 74, 88: at cultural camps, 101–4
traditional society, 3–17
trawling, 72–4
turban shells, 64
Tuross River area, 23, 24, 27
Twofold Bay, xi, 29; sealers, 17; whaling, 18–20, 35

Ulladulla, 24, 25, 72; Mickey, 28, 30
Umbarra, 92

vegetable growing, 29–30; pickers, 31–2, 45, 53, 69
Victoria, 15, 29, 96
violent conflict, 22–3
vocabulary, xi–xii, 16

117

wages and pay, 74, 98, 99; 1960s, 52–3, 61; 1970s, 64; 1980s, 71–2; licensing requirements, 64; *see also* prices
Wagonga Lands Council, 100
Wallaga Lake, 24, 27, 44, 45, 92
Wapengo, 42
water, 38, 42, 50–1; drinking vessels, 16
westerly wind, 27, 52
wet suits, 65–6
whales and whaling, 17–20, 35

white exploration and settlement, xi–xii, 12, 15–32, 35
wild cherries, 44
women; divers, 9, 37–8; in traditional society, 4–5, 6, 8, 9; kidnapping, 17
Wonboyn, 42; Disaster Bay, 11–12, 42, 49–53
wondarmas, 44
work, *see* employment and livelihood

yarns and storytelling, 6, 46–9, 102